BREEDING, WHELPING, AND NATAL CARE OF DOGS

Louis L. Vine D.V.M.

ARCO PUBLISHING COMPANY, Inc.
219 Park Avenue South, New York, N.Y. 10003

Published 1977 by Arco Publishing Company, Inc.
219 Park Avenue South, New York, N.Y. 10003

Library of Congress Cataloging in Publication Data

Vine, Louis L
  Breeding, whelping, and natal care of dogs.

  Includes index.
  SUMMARY: Deals with selective breeding, breeding,
prenatal care, whelping, postnatal care of the bitch
and puppies, and dos and don'ts of training.
  1. Dog breeding.   [1. Dog breeding]   I. Title.

SF427.2.V56   636.7′08′02   77-1817
ISBN 0-668-04152-8 (Library Edition)
ISBN 0-668-04160-9 (Paper Edition)

Printed in the United States of America

CONTENTS

INTRODUCTION

Being a foster dog parent can be one of the most satisfying experiences a dog lover can have.

Many people feel that every female dog should be bred or else she will lead an unhappy and frustrated life. This is not only untrue, but it is possible she might lead an even happier and healthier life without having puppies. When you breed your bitch you must realize that you are letting her in for a lot of pain and hard work. In many cases it comes down to the fact that the owner wants to raise a litter of puppies.

The first and most important thing to be done to attain success in raising a healthy litter of puppies is to ensure that the dam is in the best of health before she is bred.

Planned parenthood is a problem in some dogs, both females and males. Shy dogs may resist any form of the sexual act. A dog that has lived a sheltered life with his human family often does not know how to act with a dog of the opposite sex. Some sires are afraid of aggressive bitches—"women's liberation" cows them.

In problem breeders, sometimes home territory plays a role. It involves whether the sire should be taken to the dam, or vice versa. Some males/females will not perform sexually in a strange environment. Some males will not perform in the presence of any member of their human family because of having been punished for past sexual aggressiveness (such as leg riding).

During the whelping process, although the mother dog will do most of the work, the owner must be on hand and alert to any problems. Although rare, breech and other birth problems can arise. Also, when giving birth for the first time, the bitch might quite possibly, in her panic and ignorance, lie on the firstborn and smother it. Or she may not know enough to remove the sac and lick the puppy into its important first moments of life.

The difference between life and death in a puppy may be only the acute awareness of the dog owner. The early recognition of a loss in weight, restlessness, or crying in a puppy is essential in commencement of treatment for a disease or deficiency. Also, the aftercare of the mother and her puppies must be closely monitored by the owner for best health and well-being.

The early weeks of the puppies' lives—between four and 12 weeks—the socialization period—forms the temperament and personality of the adult dog. An "unhappy childhood" can ruin a sound physical specimen. Incorrigible pets are usually the result of a bad home environment.

Knowing the fundamentals of general care and nutrition may be all you will need to know. The bitch may do all the rest. Problems that do arise will require knowledge, time, and patience. In this book I shall attempt to help you be prepared for the normal as well as the abnormal situations which might arise. Your reward will be the gratification of seeing a group of healthy puppies growing up into healthy dogs.

1 PREBREEDING: SELECTIVE BREEDING

The breeding of dogs is a fascinating challenge, and an art and a gamble as well. The challenge to the breeder is to see if he can predict the resultant product of the breeding. What is hoped for is a perfectly balanced dog which meets all the breed requirements, with a good temperament and personality with all the style, spirit, and grace desirable in the particular breed. There is a further challenge that no hidden defects in the ancestry should crop up in a subsequent litter of puppies. It is incumbent on the professional dog breeder to have a complete understanding of dominant, recessive, and mixed characteristics. The same applies to the novice who seriously wishes to breed good dogs. If the novice intends to develop champions in either conformation or obedience, I heartily recommend the study of some good books on genetics.

Before any dog owner embarks on a breeding program, there are many principles of breeding that he should understand and anticipate, for the future of the individual puppy and of the breed depends on using the knowledge that is available. Many a fine family strain has been ruined by indiscriminate breeding.

Unfortunately, when a breed becomes popular, there is an influx of novices who are ignorant of the perfect specimen of the breed and haphazardly breed any two dogs so long as they have pedigree papers and possibly a few champions in their backgrounds. This is inviting disaster for the breed. Beginners must find out what a good specimen in their breed is and have a willingness to learn and study the breed and breeding per se. The learner should get to know the standards of perfection of the breed—attend many dog shows and talk with knowledgeable breeders before starting a breeding program.

A good breeder has a complete knowledge of the virtues and faults of all the ancestors of his dogs through at least 3 generations. He knows the desired and the undesired structural, temperamental, and intelligence factors of the various strains he is breeding. Good dogs are not produced by hit-and-miss breedings. They are carefully scrutinized and the faults eliminated.

A bitch and a stud don't always give to their puppies the qualities which they themselves show. They may carry many recessive characteristics which will show up in later generations.

Before setting up a breeding program, each person should have his purposes clarified in his mind. To me, there are three main things to be bred for: (1) temperament, (2) mentality, and (3) conformation—listed in my own order of priority. Certainly obedience enthusiasts are not particularly concerned with structural perfection. They are more concerned with mentality and give prime consideration to intelligence and trainability in building a particular strain. The dog-show breeder is looking for the perfect body. He is seeking to produce animals who are genetically pure for all the dominant qualities demanded by the standards of perfection of his breed. The nearer he approaches that ideal, the more similar in type will be the dogs he produces.

It is rewarding to develop puppies which are good both physically and mentally. A dog show is primarily a beauty contest in which the entrants are judged solely on their appearance and ring behavior. Obedience trials are a test of the dog owner's ability to bring out the inherent mental capabilities and intelligence of the dog. However, in my opinion temperament should not be sacrificed to intelligence or beauty.

Since I do not have the time to be a dog show exhibitor or an obedience trainer, I am more partial to a dog's temperament than to its mentality or conformation. However, I assure my readers that I am in full accord with each breed's standards of perfection and heartily endorse breeding programs headed in the direction of breeding the ideal dog and one with a high degree of intelligence.

Although this chapter is mainly devoted to the purebred dog, I am cognizant that many dogs of mixed ancestry produce highly desirable puppies, and I endorse the further breeding of any good mongrel dog if it has the personality, intelligence and body conformation that a particular owner likes. Being of mixed ancestry myself, I am entirely sympathetic to breeding dogs of mixed parentage.

TEMPERAMENT

A shy and dangerous dog, even though he may have a magnificent body, cannot live in my household.

Good temperament should be the first goal of breeders; and it should be noted in passing that although temperament is basically controlled by genetic factors, not all temperamental failings are inherited. Environment must also be considered, since experiences a dog encounters after leaving the womb affect his personality. It is often difficult to decide which traits are inherited and which are acquired. Environment versus heredity has long been disputed by psychologists and geneticists without any definite conclusions.

Non-hereditary influences on temperament include such factors as a puppy's being reared in isolation without individual care or affection, or a puppy's being the victim of bullying by larger and stronger litter mates. These conditions can affect the personality of the dog in later life and his reactions to humans—neutral, friendly, or hostile role. A nervous or shy mother can influence a puppy in later life. The mother's attitude toward humans can affect each puppy's temperament.

Every breeder should be on the lookout for timidity, fear of strangers, refusal to leave a familiar environment, sound shyness, fear of sudden changes, sight shyness, and excessive activity. Any of these signs can be inherited in the offspring and would establish abnormal traits.

Traits such as shyness or bad temper can be due to either environment or heredity. Nervous and shy dogs seem to respond to an obedience-training course; giving them pride and a sense of usefulness helps.

Seeking to control temperament in a breeding program is a complex task. Good temperament is usually present in the ancestral genes. Good temperament is dominant and will pass on to the puppies. Two dogs of good temperament may have a puppy which is not of good temperament, but if a puppy is of good temperament it will not have been bred from parents of bad temperament.

TYPES OF BREEDING

Because breeding is so complex and requires so much study, I will discuss only a few of the basic principles of the three main types: (1) inbreeding, (2) line breeding, and (3) outcrossing.

There is a fallacy among the uninformed that inbreeding and line breeding cause mental deterioration, loss of vigor, weakened constitution, structural malformation, impotency, sterility, and other weaknesses and abnormalities to appear in a breeder strain when there is too close inbreeding. This is positively not so. Inbreeding and line breeding cannot create either good or bad qualities, mental or physical. They just bring out the qualities that are already in the stock.

There is also a fallacy that puppies that are bred from father and daughter or mother and son or brother and sister are not eligible for registration. All purebred puppies are eligible for registration whether inbred, line-bred, or crossbred.

In the proper hands inbreeding and line breeding are excellent ways of helping a breed. In the wrong hands they make for deterioration of a breed. The purpose of both is to bring about breed improvement and to upgrade the stock. They make for the elimination of recessive faults and bring about purification of a strain if properly done.

Inbreeding

Inbreeding is first-generation breeding—that is, breeding father to daughter, mother to son, brother to sister, half-brother to half-sister, etcetera. It is frowned upon by many who do not understand the principles of genetics and by those who may find the moral implications shocking. The truth of the matter is that the best specimens of animals, the most beautiful, the truest in type, are gained through inbreeding.

When the breeder wants to retain as much of the blood of the sire as possible, he will often breed a daughter back to her sire. On the other hand, if it is the blood of the dam that is desired, a son is bred back to his mother. This also applies to granddaughters and grandsons.

Inbreeding is dangerous unless handled by an expert. It doubles up and intensifies all characteristics whether they be good or bad, and so the resulting puppies can have either very desirable traits or some very bad tendencies. When inbreeding, the animals must be carefully selected, as no other method of breeding equals inbreeding for intensifying the bloodline—making the best of exceptional animals—and in building a strain within a breed.

Only fault-free dogs should be mated. If there is ever any suspicion about its temperament, a dog should not be used in a breeding program. Carefully scrutinize pedigrees for at least 3 generations. Don't inbreed unless both specimens are uniform in type, size, and general appearance, are good specimens in themselves and don't have a single common outstanding major fault.

I don't advise the amateur to practice inbreeding until he is fully aware of all the principles involved.

Line Breeding

This is the mating of animals who are closely related to the same ancestors—that is, parent dogs who are closely related to a common ancestor but are not, if at all, related to each other.

The danger in line breeding occurs when selection of parents is made by pedigree alone, without considering the physical or mental traits of the mating pair. Dogs with notable faults often result. Line breeding (and inbreeding) will ensure this failure more quickly and more certainly.

Outcrossing

The bitch is bred to a male not related in any way to the many generations represented by the bitch. In other words, new bloodlines are brought into combination. Care must be taken that along with good qualities, bad ones are not introduced into the new litter. Several different types of puppies can be expected by this method, and on occasion there will be an outstanding specimen of the breed.

SELECTION OF PARENTS

This entire chapter boils down to one thing: *careful selection of parents.* In the selection of a prospective mate—bitch or stud —we must ascertain that each is as free as possible from inherited or inborn faults. The breeder must have a complete knowledge of the virtues and faults of all the ancestors for at least 3 generations so that he will know what to expect in both desired and undesired characteristics. He should fully recognize the dangers and pitfalls—and the need for using only stock which is sound in constitution, organs, and structure, and which possesses outstanding points of merit with no single fault common to the two original parents. He should be able to recognize all the shortcomings of his own dogs as well as their merits and be fully informed about their ancestors. And he should never, never mate two dogs with similar faults: the faults can be magnified many, many times in the puppies.

Unfortunately some breeders breed only to sell to the highest bidder, with little interest in breed improvement; and other breeders, hungry for stud fees, breed indiscriminately to any female presented to their studs. These practices rapidly bring about breed deterioration. The Boston bull, cocker, Airedale, boxer, German shepherd, and recently the Weimaraner, to name a few, have been injured by promiscuous and indiscriminate breeding. Fortunately these breeds have recouped under the guidance and tireless efforts of conscientious breeders.

In picking out a bitch and a sire it must be borne in mind that like produces like but that characteristics don't always blend to give the desired result. For instance, a female with a long head bred to a male with a short head may not always produce puppies with medium heads but possibly puppies with heads too long or too short.

The Brood Bitch

There is an old saying that no kennel is better than its bitches, and that is why such care must be taken in selecting the bitch in the beginning of a breeding program. One must look for a bitch of superior ancestry. The over-all quality type of the bitch is also important.

A brood bitch should be free from any inherited shyness or savageness, both of which would produce undesirable puppies. Careful selection of mates with proper temperament through several generations is the only way to eliminate these faults.

It is necessary to know how to detect a structural defect in the animal's makeup. For example, if a bitch is too long of body, she should not be bred to a male also too long of body. She should be bred with a short-bodied stud to help breed out the defect.

Size. It is thought by many that the size of the bitch determines the birth size of the puppies, but this has not been conclusively proved. Hereditary factors controlling size may be passed on by either the sire or the dam, and so people breeding a small dam to a standard size or large male can run into trouble during the whelping process. Before you mate a very small bitch, understand that the size of the puppies at birth will be governed not so much by the size of the parents as by the genetic characteristics of the puppies' ancestors.

There is a common fallacy that a small bitch mated to a large dog will produce a litter in which the female puppies will be fairly small but the males will likely be as big as, if not bigger than, their sire. Sometimes an unusually small puppy born to comparatively large parents will owe its smallness to unfavorable fetal conditions, such as poor nutritional state of the bitch or disease.

There is another belief which goes against all the principles of genetics. Some people think they can produce small puppies by withholding adequate supplies of food from the diet of a pregnant bitch. Undernourishment of the bitch to reduce the size of puppies is not the answer in a sound breeding program.

Malnutrition may stunt growth, but it will also produce unhealthy puppies.

It is believed by some that if a bitch has three or four litters sired by the same stud, each successive litter will look more like the sire and less like the dam. This belief has no scientific basis.

Telegony. Years ago it was generally believed that if a pedigreed bitch was mated with a dog of another breed or with a mongrel, she would thereafter be useless for breeding pure stock—all her subsequent litters would be mongrel or otherwise impure. Although this has been disproved, there are still people who believe it.

The Stud

In selecting a suitable stud the breeder must know the pedigree for at least 3 generations. He should also personally examine the stud and scrutinize the virtues and faults.

Get the best male available regardless of related bloodlines, and use a stud strong in characteristics in which the background of the bitch needs improvement.

Sometimes a breeder, in attempting to obtain a wanted characteristic not present in his strain, or to correct a fault he has not been able to eliminate, will use a stud possessing the desired trait but also possessing some fault. This brings undesirable characteristics out and is more likely to destroy the good traits already possessed than to add traits that are missing or desired.

It is the stud that determines the sex of the puppies as he carries the sex-determining chromosomes. Contrary to the old-age fallacy, the female, by nature of the number of ova fertilized, determines the size of the litter.

COLOR

In color inheritance there is no definite rule in genetics. The inheritance varies in each breed, with some colors dominant and others recessive. However, some colors appear to be dominant in all breeds in which they occur. These colors are brindle and black.

For example, two brindle boxers may produce a fawn puppy, whereas two fawns can never produce a brindle. Fawn to brindle breeding can produce only fawns and brindles, or all fawns, or all brindles. Brindle to brindle can produce fawns or brindles. The fact that fawn can be bred from two brindles shows that fawn is the recessive color.

Black is dominant in most breeds. Yet in other breeds, for example dachshund and basenji, red is dominant to black and tan, while in the Gordon setter, black and tan are dominant to red.

In color determination bear in mind that there is no blending of colors. For instance, a pair of black and white poodles will usually produce spotted colors and never a litter of blues.

MARKING

For an example of selective breeding for a specific marking we can discuss a collie in which a full white collar is wanted. The simplest way is to select a breeding animal in which a full white collar is well developed. This animal is mated, and the best-marked in each generation selected. In the ensuing offspring the desired collar should soon be achieved.

EYE COLOR

In certain breeds—harlequin spotted, blue merle, Great Dane, collie, Shelty, and old English sheepdog—one eye of one color and the other of another is permissible in the show ring. The color difference does not affect sight, and it is usually hereditary. Actually, however, such a dog is at a slight disadvantage in the show ring against equally good dogs with both eyes the same color.

SKIN AND COAT

Although normal and healthy in all other respects, some bitches seem to remain in a state of slight molt or shedding the year round. Scabby skin and brittle or falling-out hair may be attributed to either congenital conditions that are handed down from generation to generation or possibly to a thyroid deficiency.

If a bitch has a poor hair coat, try to mate her to a stud who has a particularly good coat and is known to have ancestors who were similarly endowed.

OTHER CHARACTERISTICS

Among characteristics which don't blend is the undershot or overshot jaw. It is a mistake to breed a bitch with an overshot jaw to a male with an undershot jaw and expect the puppies to have good mouths. The result will be puppies with overshot jaws and undershot jaws.

INBORN TRAITS AND ACQUIRED TRAITS

Inborn traits are the result of heredity. Acquired traits are not inherited by the offspring. Animals have to learn all over again the things their ancestors learned—their acquired traits—because such characteristics do not impress the brain cells of the offspring.

For example, in bird dogs, new puppies have to learn the art of hunting. Some are better hunters because they have a better sense of smell or are more intelligent and not because, as an old fallacy goes, they were whelped while the bitch was hunting. Also, puppies born to an old hunting dog are not better hunters than those born to a younger bitch; both sets of puppies contain equal hereditary traits.

As other obvious examples of non-acquired characteristics, housebroken bitches don't produce puppies that are housebroken when born; cutting the tails of puppies doesn't make succeeding generations shorter of tail; and trimming the ears of puppies doesn't lead to successive litters with smaller ears.

An ailment or disease acquired by a dog after birth is not transmitted to any offspring; for example, rickets, an ailment of the bones, is acquired and not transmitted.

HEREDITARY DISEASES:
INHERITED ABNORMALITIES

Breeding programs that have developed show dogs have also contributed to abnormalities in dogs. The veterinary profession has been becoming increasingly concerned with some of the abnormalities that dogs have been developing through generations of breeding. At a recent veterinary world congress in Paris, a resolution was unanimously adopted regarding inherited diseases. The resolution concerned the health and welfare of dogs whose breed standards hinder physiological functions of organs and parts of the body. There is an increasing list of inherited diseases which threaten health and breed improvement. Large skulls, protruding eyes, and shortened heads are among the examples cited as often being responsible for increasing the incidence of eye injury, difficult whelping, and dysfunction of the musculo-skeletal, nervous, respiratory, and cardio vascular systems.

Some abnormalities are difficult to recognize as being inherited—ulcerative colitis, hemophilia, deafness, eye diseases.

It has been proved that the incidence of hereditary disease is significantly reduced when puppies are bred from parents who show no evidence of defects. Control of hereditary diseases should be possible, therefore, by constant careful selection of breeding stock. Defective animals should be automatically disqualified from breeding, as should any animal having any association with a litter of defective animals. These animals should not be bred. They should be castrated or spayed, and can still make excellent pets. It is up to the breeder, the veterinarian, and the researcher to try to control hereditary diseases.

There are two types of hereditary abnormalities: (1) selectional abnormalities, and (2) chance abnormalities. Selectional abnormalities include all abnormalities of structure and function which are favored by the selection policy of breeders. For example, bulldog breeders deliberately select for extreme reduction of the muzzle. This leads to many problems, such as a prolonged soft palate, which causes snoring, and a short head, which causes the nasal passages to be partly or almost completely blocked

A prime example of a physical abnormality resulting from selective breeding is the collie. The skull shape has changed, from large and rectangular to a narrow, triangular-shaped head, to provide for the long pointed nose desired. This has changed both the shape of the skull cap cavity and, in my opinion, has lowered the brain capacity of some of these dogs. Several eye defects that are commonly transmitted may have resulted from the breed's narrow eyes. The old fashioned collie with his long head was much more stable and more easily trained.

Two other breeds facing possible physical ruination are the dachshund and the Welsh corgie. Only the largest and longest bodies are being bred as the long body is desirable in the show ring. Many disc problems have appeared in these breeds.

Selective breeding of thick wooly coat in poodles, kerry blues, and Bedlington terriers has produced many dogs with chronic ear problems. The hair, growing in the auditory canal and ear canal, is an excellent place for mites, bacteria and fungus to live.

Other selectional abnormalities include skinfold dermatitis as seen in English bulldog, Boston bull, pug, and Pekingese. Because of the excessive amount of wrinkling desired by breeders there is often skin irritation and infection. Entropion (inverted eyelids), ectropion (everted eyelids), and trichiasis (eyelash irritation) are other inherited abnormalities bred for.

Chance abnormalities present a different type of problem since their elimination doesn't depend on standards of breed selection. The chance abnormalities are hip dysplasia, elbow dysplasia, deafness, abnormal temperament, uterine inertia, hemophilia, cleft palate, nasal cleft, epilepsy, monorchidism and cryptorchidism, lens luxation, and retinal atrophy.

Chance Abnormalities

Hip dysplasia. This is a condition causing great concern among dog breeders. Nearly all large breeds are affected with hip dysplasia, and generally the larger the dog, the greater the chance of it. The larger breeds which mature most rapidly and grow quickly between birth and the first 3 to 4 months—usually dogs 30 pounds or over—have the highest incidense of hip dysplasia The notable exception is the greyhound; as yet hip dysplasia has not been found in the breed.

Hip dysplasia is hereditary, but it is not congenital, since the hip joints are normal at birth. Dogs confined to kennels and permitted only moderate exercise have less hip dysplasia than litter mates who are heavy and exercise a great deal. However, confinement is not the answer to prevention, as it would retard the development of intelligence and personality. It has been found that reduction of the pelvic muscle mass predisposes the puppy to hip dysplasia. This is why greyhounds have no signs of the disease; their muscles consistently have greater pelvic muscle mass than those of any other breed, and the greyhound puppy matures and takes on weight rather slowly for the first few months of life

Owing to improved skills in radiology, many cases of hip dysplasia heretofore unnoticed are now being found. Diagnosis can be done only by X ray, but not at birth. Changes in the hip are rarely present before the 8th to 20th week. A final decision about hip dysplasia cannot be made until the puppy is at least 6 to 12 months of age. I advise more than one X ray for final diagnosis.

The early symptoms of hip dysplasia are weakness and awkwardness in the hindquarters. Any persistent painful condition of the hind legs, or slowness in getting up from a reclining position, should make one suspicious of hip dysplasia and an X ray should be taken. Once a dog has hip dysplasia, the abnormality will always be present.

There is no satisfactory treatment, no medication that will cure, since the bone changes are irreversible. But there are drugs which help relieve some of the pain—aspirin, butazolidine, cortisone, and selenium compounds—and a new surgical procedure that alleviates suffering

The question that faces many dog owners, breeders, and

veterinarians is whether to destroy the dog that shows up with hip dysplasia. Not necessarily. Most dogs with hip dysplasia lead happy pain-free lives as pets, or at least a comfortable existence. If the animal has only a slight bone abnormality, obedience training and hunting may be allowed so long as there is no evidence of pain. Strenuous and fatiguing exercise should be avoided.

While the pet dog can lead a normal life with hip dysplasia, the breeder is the key to prevention and control of the disease. No one should ever breed a dog with hip dysplasia, even though he may feel justified in breeding the affected animal in order to preserve certain bloodlines to maintain quality, intelligence, disposition, conformation, or behavior.

As part of a control program for hip dysplasia, the Orthopedic Foundation for Animals has been formed. The owner of an animal who wishes to have a dog certified as free from hip disease writes to the OFA at P.O. Box 8251, Philadelphia, for application forms and instructions for submitting pelvic photographs. The X rays are scrutinized by a team of experts who classify the animal in one of three categories, normal, near-normal, or dysplastic. Any breeder wishing to embark on a sound breeding program should submit X rays to his veterinarian or to the OFA for consultation. There is no place for hip dysplasia in selective breeding.

Elbow dysplasia. This is a deformity of the elbow joint. It is similar to hip dysplasia and causes a lameness. Such an animal should not be bred.

Patella dysplasia. Many small breeds have a recurring dislocation of the knee. It is seen most often in chihuahuas, poodles, and Pomeranians. It can be treated surgically, but the offspring will be subject to this inconvenience.

Harelip and cleft palate. With modern advances in medicine and surgery, these conditions can be corrected surgically. Although it has been a universal custom to dispose of young puppies born with these abnormalities, with careful nursing most of them can be saved. But they should not be bred, because of the possibility of the defect being transmitted to their offspring. The abnormalities are most common in the Boston terrier, cocker, beagle, and Norwegian elkhound.

Monorchidism and *cryptorchidism.* These are hereditary defects in which one or both testes don't descend to the normal position in the scrotum. When both testicles are involved, the dog is usually sterile. Although a dog with one testicle can be a successful sire, because of the hereditary nature of the defect breeding is not recommended. The dog may have an unreliable disposition; also, the testicles are prone to tumors. The AKC disqualifies any animal with monorchidism or cryptorchidism; and the only way the defects can be controlled is by elimination of such dogs from any breeding program, and of any dogs in whose pedigrees it has appeared.

The defects are most often found in the toy breeds. They appear to be recessive—that is, normal males can sire both normal and affected males out of bitches born of normal sires and normal grandsires. The idea that the defects are sex-linked (like hemophilia) is popular but has not been proved or disproved.

In treatment some veterinarians administer hormones to help the testes descend to their normal position. The value of this therapy is questionable.

Hemophilia. This is another hereditary disease; and there are two types in dogs. The disease results in a subcutaneous bleeding after minor injury and excessive hemorrhaging after wounds. It is similar to hemophilia in humans in that the blood doesn't contain all the necessary elements for clotting. In dogs as in humans, it is the female who carries the disease and the male who becomes the bleeder. Certain breeds, such as the Irish setter and the basenji, seem to be afflicted.

Cystinura. This inherited abnormality is seen mainly in Dalmatians. It is a tendency to form urinary stones. The exact nature of the biochemical defect is unknown, but we know that there is a tendency for it to be transmitted genetically.

Achondroplasia (the "swimmer"). The puppies cannot stand, but move around like turtles with all four legs extended outward. It is a condition in which the bones don't harden properly. It occurs most often in such breeds as Pekingese, bulldog, Scottish terrier, and Sealyham—breeds with short, thick legs and heavy muscles.

Diagnosis can be confirmed by X ray.

There is no cure, and it is best to destroy all affected puppies. However, with proper mineral and vitamin supplements, sometimes a puppy will develop sufficiently to get on his feet, although weeks later than his litter mates, and sometimes will even catch up in size. The gait has a telltale stiffness.

Some experienced breeders have been successful in having these animals recover by the age of 6 to 7 weeks by giving them a rough bed of blanket or sacking and an old piece of carpet on the floor of the pen, with nothing smooth or slippery under them.

But even if a puppy does survive and grow stronger as he gets older, it is a genetic defect, and he would be detrimental to a breeding program.

Congenital Abnormalities

Cranioschisis (soft spots on the head). This is a condition in which the bones are not closed at birth. It is common in the toy breeds, especially the chihuahau. Normally the spaces close by the time the animal is 3 to 4 months old, but occasionally an animal will go through life with a small unclosed area. There is no pathological significance to the soft spots; the animal may lead a healthy life with the unformed bones in his head.

Hydrocephalus. This is "water on the brain." The entire head is enlarged. It is not considered a hereditary defect, although it occurs more commonly in certain breeds.

In puppies and young dogs there are two congenital abnormalities which cause persistent vomiting. Diagnosis is made with barium X rays:

Esophageal obstruction or *dilation*. This results from a congenital malformation within the chest. It obstructs food from passing down into the stomach. It is difficult to treat, and surgery is the only solution.

Pyloric stenosis. This arises from a congenital stricture of the pyloris (outlet of the stomach). Solid food collects in the stomach and is unable to pass through the narrow outlet valve. This mass is eventually vomited, depriving the puppy of the nutrients necessary for survival. A careful dietary program of soft semi-liquid cereals is an absolute necessity. In severe cases surgery is the only solution.

Familial renal disease. This is a rather rare inherited kidney disease in Norwegian elkhounds. It occurs in young animals and causes uremia.

THE CANINE EYE AND SELECTIVE BREEDING

Breed Traditions

Some breed traditions in the canine eye are from antiquity. The St. Bernard has the weeping eye. The cocker spaniel has the soulful, watery eye. The Pekingese has the eye of mystery. The Boston has the large eye of play. The bulldog has the round fearful eye. The setter has the soft, mild eye. The fox terrier has the shoe-button eye of mischief. The bull terrier has the devil-may-care eye. And the chowchow—the Chinese dog—has the almond-shaped eye.

Hereditary Diseases

Just as there are breed traditions, there are indicated breed tendencies in eye diseases. Eye diseases have been found in 60 breeds. Ectropion (everted eyelids) has been reported in 25 breeds, with the bloodhound and St. Bernard most commonly affected. Entropion (inverted eyelids) is associated with chihuahuas. Trichiasis (abnormal growth and irritation of the eyelashes) is found most often in cocker spaniels and bulldogs Lens luxation (dislocation of the lens) is seen mainly in wire-haired terriers and Sealyhams.

One of the most rapidly increasing and devastating eye dis-

plication because of a cataract which usually accompanies PRA). The other breeds most often affected are the rough collie, Labrador retriever, cocker and springer spaniels, Cairn terrier, and miniature long-haired dachshund. It is a degenerative disease for which there is no effective treatment and which inevitably causes total blindness.

One of the reasons for the spread of PRA is that it occurs well after a dog has reached maturity and may have been bred and produced many litters before it is diagnosed. The average age of onset in poodles is 4½ years; the range is usually between 4 and 6 years. Selective breeding is the only answer. No dog diagnosed as having PRA should ever be used for breeding stock, and no matron or sire who has ever produced a puppy with PRA should ever be used for breeding.

Another prominent hereditary disease is the collie ectasia syndrome, which can generally be recognized in a 6-week old puppy. Since it is a congenital abnormality, it is dangerous to breed collies with even a minimal lesion, since this can spread to the puppies. It usually results in total blindness.

Other hereditary conditions of the eye are the wall eye in collies and Great Danes, and prolapse of the third eyelid seen in bulldogs, bull terriers, and spaniels.

BIRTH CONTROL

In this age of overpopulation in the pet world, birth control is very significant. Spaying or castration are the most common methods, but others are not to be ruled out. Birth control pills (hormonal steroids) can be used for inhibition of heat and mating. Estrogens can be used to abort pregnancy. Vasectomy in the male can also be utilized. IUD plastic devices, "morning after" pills, and a birth control vaccine are being tested for use.

A new birth control method has been devised by a couple of Italian researchers. They inject a non-hormonal compound into the bitch which produces resorption of the fetus during the first half of gestation and resorption or expulsion of the fetus during the latter part of pregnancy. The bitches which had aborted with this injection returned to estrus within normal intervals of time, exhibited normal mating behavior, were fertile, and delivered normal puppies.

2 BREEDING

The commonest mistake that the novice breeder makes is to put a bitch and a stud together in a room and leave them alone to let nature take its course. This is assumed to ensure a litter of puppies. In the main it is a faulty premise, and breeding would be strictly a gamble following this procedure. Although normal healthy animals would be expected to be able to mate with alacrity under the circumstances, our "civilized" dogs are prone to problems, and there are many factors to be considered before conception can take place and a successful program begun.

SEXUAL MATURITY OF THE STUD

The male dog reaches sexual maturity anywhere from 6 months of age in the small breeds to 1 up to 1½ years in the large breeds. The larger the breed, the slower the maturity. An unscientific way of deciding when a male dog is ready for breeding is setting it at the moment he lifts a leg to urinate and has "become a man."

It is not a good idea to use a young stud on a regular basis until he has reached his full maturity. I don't advise using a stud, except under unusual circumstances, under 1 year of age, and in the large breeds, for example Great Dane and St. Bernard, I would say they are 1½ years old before they reach full maturity.

A stud should have a physical examination before he is bred. Particularly the semen should be examined to be sure that he can sire a litter. He should be examined for intestinal parasites, because he should be in good health. Also, for the older male dog a day or two before he is scheduled to mate, male-hormone injections will increase his libido.

SEXUAL MATURITY OF THE BITCH

Heat, or estrus, is nature's signal that the bitch is ready to mate. It is commonly described as being "in season." The bitch will begin licking her vulva preceding her heat cycle, and this is a good indication that the season is not far off.

The first period of heat usually occurs anywhere after 6 months of age, up to 12 months, depending on the breed. In the smaller breeds, such as the toys, the heat period can come any time after 6 months—usually 7 to 9 months. In the larger breeds—German shepherd, boxer, etcetera—it usually comes at 10 to 12 months. However, it varies with the individual and with the season of the year. It seems that spring and fall are most conducive to the sex life of animals. There have been some unusual cases of dogs coming into their first heat at 5 months of age and others not until 18 months of age.

As a rule the first heat is agreed upon as not the best time to breed a bitch. Usually she is not quite mature, and most breeders and veterinarians advise waiting for the second period at least.

A physical examination must be done on the brood bitch before attempting to breed her. It is not uncommon to find an extremely small vagina in a maiden bitch. The vagina does not enlarge properly in the heat cycle for natural breeding to be culminated. The veterinarian can dilate it, with or without anesthetic, depending on the size. The physical examination should include testing for parasites because bitches who are anemic or just recovering from a debilitating disease may not be good brood bitches.

HEAT CYCLE OF THE BITCH

The commonest cause of unsatisfactory or incomplete mating is attempting to breed at the wrong time of the estrus cycle. Consequently a complete understanding of the cycle is primary in establishing a breeding program.

The beginning of the estrus cycle, called the proestrus, is signified by a discharge from the vulva. Actually at first there is a slight white or yellowish discharge, and then the heat period, or proestrus, begins, with the appearance of a bloody discharge and swelling of the vagina. The proestrus blood usually continues from 7 to 9 days, in a normal dog, but it can vary anywhere from 2 to 27 days in some irregular cycles. During this period the bitch generally has a hostile attitude toward males. At the end of the proestrus period her attitude changes, and she becomes interested in the other sex, attempting to attract them and often mounting them in a teasing fashion.

The average duration of proestrus is about 9 days, but in an abnormal cycle it may last from 8 to 24 days.

The heat period usually comes every 6 months, but no bitch can be counted on to be exactly 6 months to the day. Several factors such as time of year and emotional state have a bearing on the heat cycle.

The optimum time to breed is about 24 to 48 hours after ovulation, and ovulation will usually commence 9 to 12 days after the first sign of blood, in a normal female. Usually a bitch will accept the male only during the middle part of her estrus. Most breeders consider the 13th day the best breeding day, but some bitches will accept the male after 8 days and some will wait until 14 or 15 days. It has been recorded that some bitches have bred on the 5th day after the first sign of blood and others have gone as long as the 25th day.

A good barometer of the correct time to breed is a change in blood color to pale red or pale yellow. At this point the congestion around the vulva has decreased, redness has begun to leave, and although the vulva is still swollen, it has become soft and pliable. The best indication of the readiness and willingness of the bitch is when she puts her tail aside and extends her vulva.

Many amateur breeders fail to ascertain the correct time and breed either too early or too late. The veterinarian has a vaginal-smear test for determining ovulation in the bitch. Knowledge of the approximate time of ovulation is essential in a productive breeding program, especially with bitches who have abnormal cycles and don't accept the male at the normal time. Although no test can fix the exact time for breeding, vaginal smears can be used to closely estimate the time of ovulation. When the shipping time for a female is critical, when a female has shown abnormal heat periods, or to avoid overworking a valuable stud, a vaginal smear should be done at regular intervals, at least every 48 hours.

There is another ovulation test, which determines the glucose contents of the cervical mucus. Strips of paper are introduced into the vagina, and by a change in color they indicate that glucose is present. This is a sign that ovulation is taking place. These indicator strips are the same as those used in the routine examination for urine and are easily obtainable from any laboratory-supply company.

There are people who use estrogens and other hormones to bring their dogs into heat. They also use hormone preparations to produce large litters of puppies. I am against hormones for these purposes, as their misuse may damage a good bitch for life. Many times hormones are given to bring the female into heat in her off season, and this is unsuccessful most of the time because ovulation does not take place without further stimulation by hormones.

Irregular Heat Periods

If a bitch remains a maiden for a long time after full maturity, she may have irregular seasons. However, after she is mated and has proved fertile, she may have normal intervals between her heat periods.

As the bitch gets older her heat cycles become less regular, and this is one of the first signs of old age. Some old dogs come into heat only every year or two, much to the delight of their owners. As the dog gets older she may show signs of heat but may not be capable of conceiving, because she doesn't ovulate. This is also true in "false heat" periods, during which a bitch goes through the full symptoms of estrus, such as bleeding, enlarged vulva, and attraction of males, but are not ovulating and conception is impossible. I have seen bitches 15 to 18 years old with false heat periods attracting males as if they were young and pretty maidens.

Prolonged Heat Periods

Some bitches stay in heat longer than the normal 3-week period. This is usually abnormal, although some maiden bitches, in heat for the first time, will stay in estrus 4 to 5 weeks without any abnormal body changes. A prolonged heat period is usually caused by some abnormal factor.

Infection of the uterus can give all the external signs of a heat period, including attracting all the males in the neighborhood. A bladder infection which causes irritation and bleeding of the vaginal tract can also sometimes be misinterpreted as a heat period.

When there is a prolonged heat period, the bitch should be examined by a veterinarian to find out what is causing the condition.

I advise against attempting to breed any female with an abnormal or prolonged heat period; and the life of a bitch should not be endangered by forcing her to breed with a male while she is suffering from some female irregularity.

Silent Heat Periods

This is an abnormal type of period in which the bitch does not show any of the signs of estrus. Although she is willing to accept a male, she will be in and out of season before she can be bred.

This is a bitch who requires professional help. I personally advise vaginal smears at monthly intervals to determine the health of her female organs, when she is in estrus, and when ovulation will occur. The condition is usually caused by a hormonal imbalance and is difficult to treat.

I would be cautious of using such an animal in a breeding program because there is a probability that the condition is hereditary.

Other Abnormalites

Some bitches will breed from practically the first day in season until the last. A stud cannot tell when she is ovulating, and there will be males around her during her entire heat cycle. These are abnormal females with abnormal tendencies, and they should not be bred.

THE SPERM: EJACULATION

In a normal mating the male ejaculates many thousands of sperm cells, and although only one is needed to fertilize each egg of the female, it is assumed that the more sperm present, the more likelihood there is of the egg cells being fertilized. The quantity of sperm cells and their health and vitality, together with the number of ova shed by the female during her heat cycle, determine the size of the litter.

The ejaculated fluid consists of three fractions. The first fraction, which contains no sperm, takes about half a minute to be voided. It is a clear fluid from the glands of the urethra. The second fraction is the sperm and takes only 1 to 2 minutes to be ejaculated. The third fraction, which contains no sperm, takes from 5 to 30 minutes to be voided. It is fluid from the prostate gland and is usually what the male ejaculates while he is tied to the female. While the third fraction is not necessary for conception, it serves as bulk to be washed forward into the uterus. When the first two fractions have been deposited in the vagina, there is a good chance of conception even though mating may have lasted only 1½ minutes, or long enough for the second fraction to have occurred.

THE TIE

The purpose of the tie in dogs is not fully understood, although a number of theories and explanations have been put forward. It doesn't seem to have any special significance in the present-day domestic dog.

Unlike what happens in other mammals, the dog's ejaculation doesn't occur until after penetration into the vagina and the greatly enlarged glands of the penis is held firmly in place by the contractor muscles of the vagina.

Normally the tie lasts from 5 to 30 minutes, and the time has no particular significance or influence on conception or on the number of puppies that result. Any time over 30 minutes is abnormal; if it is more than 45 minutes, a veterinarian should be consulted.

It is best to leave the dogs in a quiet, relaxed position while they are tied together. The male may turn around so that he is headed in the opposite direction of the bitch, so that the two animals are rear to rear. By all means never try to pull them apart, as you might injure either or both of them. And *never, never* pour cold water over them or try to beat them apart. It is heartless and cruel to try to separate them before their bodies are ready to release them from their love union. Trying to separate them just terrifies them and often injures them. The quieter they are left, the sooner they will separate.

There are many fallacies concerning the tie, and I know one breeder who times the tie, claiming that for every 3 minutes the animals are tied together there is another puppy conceived. This is absolutely false, since ejaculation of the sperm takes only from 1 to 1½ minutes.

SEXUAL BEHAVIOR PATTERNS

According to the ancestry of the dog, certain breeds were pack hunters and strictly monogamous. They stayed with one female completely and bred only with her. Dogs who claim the wolf as their procreator seem to be in this group. The rest of dogdom, which goes back to the jackal, has different behavior patterns.

Samoyedes, chowchows, Eskimo dogs, huskies, and Russian laikas are definitely linked to the northern wolf. The males of the wolf breeds will extend courtesies only to females in the same pack while they will fight off female dogs of other breeds and other packs.

Most other breeds are descendants of the jackal. These males are courteous and gentlemanly to every female they encounter.

Through the generations domestication has relaxed the morals, and most males will breed with any females that allow them to. Most stud dogs today are of the "cave-man" type and will force their attention on any bitches presented to them.

Most bitches resent forced attention and have to be restrained or given tranquilizers. Many a bitch will fight off one male but readily accept the mating advances of another. Some bitches enjoy playing hard to get. It is common for a highly pedigreed bitch to fight off an equally highly pedigreed stud—absolutely refuse to be serviced by him—and readily accept a mongrel in the neighborhood whom she has fallen for.

NATURAL BREEDING AND PROBLEMS

A common mistake made by novice breeders is to throw two dogs together who have never met before and then expect a successful breeding. Certainly dogs can breed by themselves, and especially can any dog that roams the streets accomplish this natural act without any outside interference. However, because of the confinement that most pet dogs have nowadays, and their close relationships with their owners, they have been inhibited from some of their natural instincts, such as the procedure of breeding—and many of them need help. I've seen male dogs mount bitches heads in pure ignorance of how to perform the act. Likewise, many females require tranquilizers to calm them down; they are terrified by male dogs attempting to make love to them.

The two most necessary requisites for a successful union are a stud who is keen and persistent and able to make a successful union, and a bitch at the correct stage of her estrus and willing. If the breeder attempts mating too early in the heat cycle, the bitch will usually be overaggressive toward the male and will growl and bite him. This will decrease his desire, and a young inexperienced male might be ruined for life as a stud.

We must have appropriate surroundings for the mating, that the bitch and male are accustomed to, or at least not frightened by. They should not be thrown into the room and expected to breed immediately. Their introduction should be correct and proper, and they should be allowed to have some sexual foreplay so that they may become accustomed to each other and increase their sexual excitement.

Although they should be allowed to be alone so that they can play and tease each other in an uninhibited way, I recommend that they be watched from the outside so that there can be assurance that the union has taken place and so that when problems are encountered someone will be available to help the dogs. Most breeders and veterinarians connected with dog breeding are aware of the many difficulties that can be encountered in mating. Many dogs will not mate if there is someone in the room with them. Some males will allow help in mounting and penetration; other males will stop as soon as outside help is attempted. Each case has to be handled separately.

Shy and timid females may be helped by tranquilizers. Massaging the prostate, and hormone shots, are of some help in the male who is timid or does not show desire.

If the male is too aggressive and frightens the bitch, someone should immediately step in and help.

For aggressive bitches help is needed by two or more people. I usually have the owner hold the bitch's head, sometimes using a muzzle to prevent her from biting when the male penetrates. I also have someone hold the bitch's legs up so she will not sit down when the male attempts to mount her. The same procedure applies for a stubborn bitch.

In large breeds—St. Bernards or Great Danes—I have used four or five soft-drink crates under their middles to prevent them from sitting down.

In breeding large bitches to small studs, or vice versa, we use large books for the animals to stand on so that their sizes will coincide. It is also necessary to have something non-slippery, such as rubber matting, for the animals to stand on.

Many a willing female turns frigid when the male penetrates her vagina for the first time because of excruciating pain due to her very narrow female organs. Thereafter when he attempts to mount her, she will not tolerate it and sits on the floor. I can't emphasize too strongly that all virgin bitches should have a vaginal examination before breeding, with dilation if needed.

NUMBER OF MATINGS PER LITTER

In the mating of dogs most breeders agree that 2 or 3 matings are desired, although one is all that is necessary. It is good to breed 2 or 3 times for several reasons: to ensure the bitch's being served during the period of ovulation, which sometimes is difficult to ascertain; it gives the bitch the best opportunity to produce the largest number of puppies; and it gives the stud a chance to produce some good sperm if he has not been used for some time. It has been proved that if a stud is not used for a long period, the semen may lose much of its potency.

I don't advise breeding more than 4 or 5 days apart because of the possibility of conception at both breedings, and there will then be a premature puppy or two in a litter of normal healthy puppies.

More than one male can breed with a female, and she can have puppies by each of the studs. For this reason some litters are composed of many different colors, sizes, and shapes of puppies. The bitch, after a night on the town, can give birth to many different types of puppies.

AFTER MATING

It is the opinion of many experts that for at least 10 days after the bitch has been mated, she should not be moved into a new kennel or alongside a male other than the one who serviced her. It is believed that disturbing environmental conditions can possibly be the cause of abortion in some bitches, especially highly excitable and nervous ones.

MISMATING OF A BITCH

Accidents indeed do happen. Occasionally a bitch escapes from her confinement and is bred by a neighborhood Casanova. To avoid the whelping of undesirable puppies, the mismating can be aborted.

If the misalliance is immediately apprehended—within an hour—douching the bitch with cold water and vinegar (half and half) is an effective method of avoiding pregnancy. It must be done within an hour after breeding, before the sperm has had a chance to fertilize any eggs high in the uterus.

There is a method that is almost 100 percent successful if done within a week of breeding. It must be done by a professional. It is a female-hormone injection, and the earlier it is given, the more effective it is. The only disadvantage is that it prolongs the heat cycle a week to 10 days. Most people don't mind under the circumstances.

Another procedure, but which is rather risky and should also be done by a professional, is an intravaginal injection of ether. This must be performed within 24 to 48 hours following mating.

There is a drug called Malucidin which is used in advanced cases of pregnancy. It is injected prior to the 44th day of pregnancy and will dissolve fetuses within 48 to 60 hours. However, it entails danger to the bitch, and I personally would not use it unless the pregnancy was detrimental to the life of the bitch.

ARTIFICIAL INSEMINATION

Artificial insemination in dogs has been used for about twenty years. The AKC requires a veterinarian's certificate of confirmation regarding the breeding. Actually the procedure *should* be performed by a veterinarian, as many laymen have produced uterine infection in their bitches.

Where natural breeding cannot be accomplished, artificial insemination should be attempted. I would recommend artificial breeding to any breeder who is not successful with a problem bitch, but certainly natural copulation should be attempted first. Also, it is possible through artificial insemination for a stud in one part of the country to breed with a bitch in another part of the country. Frozen semen is now available for that purpose.

The technique involves depositing the semen, with a syringe, into and through the cervix. Conditions must be absolutely perfect; correct temperature of the syringe and the absence of any sperm-killing chemicals are among the primary requisites for successful results.

FERTILITY AND STERILITY IN THE BITCH

Any breeding program suffers a serious setback when no puppies are produced. The breeder is completely reliant on the quantity and quality of puppies produced from the union of male and female. In the production of puppies, without a doubt the commonest cause of sterility in the female is failure of the owner to present her for service at the right time of the estrus cycle There are many factors which affect the fertility of the bitch, and her sterility can often be traced to the owner's ignorance of her dietary needs, her emotional problems, and her physical well-being.

A well-balanced diet is essential for the proper functioning of the bitch's body. Often an adjustment in diet will allow a sterile dog to produce puppies.

Sterility is often due to emotional or psychological factors. Often the bitch shows aversion or hesitation when a male approaches her. Bitches have their likes and dislikes, and one male may be refused but another perfectly acceptable. Sympathy and understanding are needed in treatment.

Environmental conditions can affect the bitch's fertility. Sometimes moving the bitch to a strange place and climate will affect her physiological and emotional balances. Often bitches shipped to faraway places will not breed, but in the confines of their own neighborhood will breed with the first male that makes them an offer. Before breeding, a dog should be allowed time to adjust to a new environment and climate.

Physical causes of barrenness in bitches include such things as poor hormonal production, blockage of the Fallopian tubes, a thick and tough hymen, and a juvenile vagina which is small and constricted.

Poor hormonal production often responds to hormone therapy with good results. Conditions such as failure to come into normal heat, frigidity, and abnormally long heat periods can often be corrected by hormone treatment. However, the careless use of hormones can do more harm than good, and the method should be left to the discretion of a veterinarian. The most effective hormones are those which are similarly used in humans to help ovulation—fertility drugs. Such other drugs as cortisones and thyroids should be used only on the advice of a veterinarian.

Bacterial infections, tumor formations, or any serious illness usually will result in temporary or permanent sterility. Infections which may result in sterility are metritis, vaginitis, and ovarian cysts. Tumors found in the vaginal passageway can be corrected by surgery, and the bitch will then conceive.

Cystic ovaries cause nymphomania by keeping the bitch in constant heat. Most of the time she is nervous, high-strung, ill-tempered, and inclined to fight both males and other bitches. This condition usually requires surgery on one or both ovaries. If only one ovary is affected, removal would still allow normal heat cycles and the bitch would be able to conceive and produce normal litters. If both ovaries are affected, complete hysterectomy is the only answer.

There is a bacterial infection which causes sterility in bitches. A bitch may appear in excellent health and may even have a normal heat period (or a short period or none at all). There may be a normal mating, but it will result in either failure to conceive, abortion, or puppies that die shortly after birth. The veterinarian can detect the infection with a vaginal smear, and treatment is with antibiotics. If complete recovery is effective, it may be possible to breed the animal in the future.

After a serious disease, such as distemper, a young bitch may become temporarily sterile for up to 2 years. However, if the animal recovers completely, the tissues of her female organs will usually revert to healthy functioning tissue and she will have normal reproductive cycles.

There is sometimes a temporary barrier in breeding due to an acid secretion in the bitch which neutralizes the male sperm. This secretion has not been fully comprehended and can be due to a disease of the uterus or a "lethal factor" in the vaginal lubricant of some bitches. It can exert its influence on the sperm within 16 seconds after the sperm is exposed to the vaginal contents. This acidic condition can be tested for by inserting blue litmus test paper into the vagina. For a bitch with this condition (paper turns red) I advise a douche with bicarbonate of soda solution one hour prior to breeding.

Poor health due to heavy worm infestation can hinder pregnancy.

A very fat bitch will often fail to conceive, and if she does she will be subject to uterine inertia or a difficult whelping. It is obvious that proper diet and exercise will possibly correct this type of infertility. It is bad policy to breed a fat bitch.

The Age of the Bitch

Because the number of eggs shed by the ovaries during the heat period affects the efficiency of the bitch's reproductive organs, as she gets older and her ability to produce eggs decreases she declines to complete sterility. Usually the first sign of approaching sterility in older age is the commencement of irregular heat cycles. Also, as she gets older the bitch is more prone to female disorders due to hormonal dysfunction.

There is a common fallacy that if a bitch is bred at least once in her young life, she will be immune from such female disorders as infections and tumors in her old age. This is not true; it has been proved that dogs that are not bred are usually less likely to develop growths, cysts, and tumors than the brood bitch.

There are several diseases that aging bitches may endure which cause sterility. One of these is pyometra, which is pus formation in the uterine tract.

Another is metritis—a dangerous condition. It is usually seen in middle-aged and older dogs following a heat period. This is a time for the owner to be especially aware of any fever or general lethargy in a female dog; and immediate professional help is needed to save her. In severe cases the only cure is surgery to remove the infected uterus before general blood poisoning occurs.

My personal feeling is that after a brood bitch has completed her productive years, she should have a complete hysterectomy so that she will not suffer in her later years from female disorders. I especially recommend this to owners who have bitches that are also valued pets or companions. It prevents trouble later in life, when surgery would be more dangerous.

Breeding Span in Bitches

The breeding span varies in female dogs according to many factors. A bitch may have a short breeding span due to ill health, bad rearing, or environmental changes. Sexual puberty is delayed in some females because of ill health, bad rearing, emotional changes in environment, arrested growth, or poor nutrition. Also, in the old dog the extent of the span varies. When the bitch stops coming into heat can be affected by climate, environmental conditions, housing, feeding, hormonal disturbances, and even temperament.

FERTILITY AND STERILITY IN THE STUD

Sterility in the male can be due to a variety of causes. Some can be helped by veterinary intervention, while others are impossible to cure. Degrees of infertility may be inherited; the potency of the stud dog seems to run in certain families. There are some studs who for generations have been known to throw large and healthy litters. This is a good reason for knowing the ancestry in a breeding program.

Some males' sperm is weak, immobile, or even absent. A microscopic examination by a veterinarian can easily tell the exact status of the sperm, and whether the dog is likely to be a good stud.

There is a condition, called phimosis, in male dogs in which they cannot extend the penis from the sheath. It is due to a tight ligament. Sugery gives good results, and dogs can be bred soon after.

Monorchids and cryptorchids are often sterile. Although it is not a good idea to breed such dogs, because the condition can be inherited, if there is one testicle it can be functioning normally. If both testicles are hidden inside the abdomen, the dog is usually lacking in viable sperm.

Canine brucellosis is a newly recognized disease which causes infection and sterility in males. It can be considered a canine venereal disease because it is contracted during sexual intercourse. It originates as an acidic condition in the bitch which kills the sperm. The male can be contaminated by such a bitch and can pass the infection on to other bitches whom he services. It causes an enlargement and then shrinking of the testicles, and skin infection on the scrotum. A purulent discharge from the penis may or may not be present. If the infection is found in time, it can be treated with antibiotics and will not have a sterilizing effect on the male.

Another cause of sterility can be a serious illness. Any serious illness in the male can affect sperm production. This is usually only temporary. After a long period of convalescence, with proper care, the male is usually restored to his full fertility.

Too frequent breeding, underfeeding, lack of excercise, and confinement are all causes of sterility. Any stud used frequently should be kept on a high-animal-protein diet, with plenty of outdoor exercise and freedom. Close confinement and environmental conditions affect the nervous temperament of the dog. An extremely nervous stud may not father many good litters. Faulty nutrition usually deprives the stud of the vitamins important is sperm production. The male may have millions of sperm in his ejaculation, but if they are weak and anatomically deformed, they cannot reach the ova in the uterus and usually conception cannot take place. It has been found by researchers that the male is usually to blame in about half the failures in production of puppies.

Many dog breeders like to breed their studs not later than in the latter part of the adolescent period mainly because they want the dog to have experience in the act of breeding. It is astonishing how many of our house pets are ignorant of the mechanics of mating and often have to be shown. Once they are shown the proper way, there's no stopping them, and they do quite well by themselves. There are some male house pets who show absolutely no interest in female dogs although they get terribly interested in pillows and other objects around the house. These dogs may be in good health and produce good sperm, but they have no interest in the opposite sex. Their abnormal behavior follows psychological factors, which usually are a combination of hereditary indifference and rearing in an artificial environment. These shy breeders are usually pets who have had little contact with other dogs because they have not been allowed to roam around. They usually prefer the company of humans. Occasionally I've resorted to male-hormone injections to help the sexual drive.

Frequency of Use

Frequency of use varies with the health of the stud and the quality and quantity of his sperm. Most normal virile males can be used at least twice a week without any harm to health or decline in fertility. In dogs with a lower fertility rate, once in 2 weeks may deplete the body of active sperm.

It is recommended that a stud be used often, at regular intervals, rather than trying to conserve his potency by breeding him only rarely.

The Age of the Stud

As the stud gets older his fertility usually diminishes because of interference and reduction in sperm production. The quantity and quality of sperm cells affect the conception rate because the sperm have a long way to go through the vaginal passage into the uterus to reach the ova.

Most males if kept in good health are fertile until 7 to 8 years of age. After that time sperm production begins to wane, and although a dog may sire litters, he may need help with extra amounts of food and hormone therapy.

A male in poor health, even because of a severe infestation of worms, can be reduced in potency and his value as a stud threatened.

Although the number of puppies in a litter sired by an old dog may be smaller, it is a fallacy that the quality will be poorer. Once the sperm makes contact with the ova, no matter how old the stud, the puppies will be of the same quality and have the same good points (and bad) as if the sire were only one year of age. The factors transmitted by him to his offspring are genetic and are not affected by his age.

Another fallacy is that unless a stud is used when he is young, he will be impotent in later years. Many males not bred before 3 or 4 years of age have sired full litters. If a male is in good condition, his potency is available for many years without his ever having been used as a stud.

MEDICINAL SPAYING

In recent years there have been hormonal drugs on the market to prevent a female from coming into heat. They have been used on countless thousands of dogs and to some extent are still being used. However, the United States government has taken them off the market for general use because too many complications were being noted. Many dogs became sterile and were never able to conceive. Many dogs developed infections of the uterus, such as metritis, and hysterectomy was necessary. I'm sure that in the near future there will be an effective birth-control measure available, but at the present time the human birth-control pills are not satisfactory for an effective birth-control program in dogs.

There are many preparations on the market, with names such as "Anti-Mate," which are supposed to help destroy the odor that attracts males. They are basically of chlorophyll derivation. For household pets there are little sanitary pads that are strapped to the animal's body and these help keep blood from spotting the house. I would not depend on any of these products 100 percent in preventing the mismating of a bitch.

It should be borne in mind that some bitches in heat are anxious to escape from their maximum security to join males on the outside. They will even dig under or through doors to gain their freedom. Likewise, male dogs will go through brick walls to get to their ladies in heat.

SEX AND SIZE OF LITTERS

There are two erroneous beliefs which some breeders stubbornly stick to. Some believe that the sexes in a litter depend to a large extent on the stage in the heat period during which the dam was mated. For instance, they believe that if a mating is made at a later time in the estrus cycle, more males will be delivered, and that if more females are wanted, service should be arranged early in the heat period. The other belief is that the age of the parents has a determining influence on the sex of the offspring. It is believed that with older parents male puppies are more likely to be born, and the younger the bitch or stud the more females will be born. Actually the sex of the puppies is fixed the moment a sperm unites with the egg during conception.

I have had breeders tell me that they can predict the sex of puppies according to the direction in which the animals were facing during conception. Facing to the east means more females, and in any other direction there will be more male dogs.

According to my knowledge, raising puppies with sex control in mind is not possible at the present time. But with the research in progress it would not surprise me if in the near future we can control sex in puppies.

It has been proved that litter size seems to run in certain

family strains, and so it is advisable to breed dogs whose ancestry shows large litters if such are desired. However, too large a litter can affect the size and health of the puppies and often affect the health of the mother, who in some cases may require outside help in feeding and rearing the puppies.

SUMMARY: THE BITCH

1. Don't breed a bitch under a year of age; it is much better to wait until she is 18 months of age so that she is physically developed and mature.

2. Don't breed a bitch with physical defects or one who is shy or has a bad disposition.

3. Don't breed a bitch who has serious faults according to the standards of the breed.

4. Don't breed a bitch who is in poor condition, either recuperating from a serious illness or from a heavy infestation of worms, or who is nutritionally deficient.

5. See that the bitch has a complete physical checkup before breeding her to make sure she is free from worms and other parasites, is free from disorders of the body, such as female infections, and is anatomically able to accept a male.

6. Don't breed a bitch unless you are ready and willing to lose a few nights' sleep and to take care of puppies until they are ready for their new owners.

SUMMARY: THE STUD

1. Don't breed a stud on a regular basis until he has reached full sexual maturity.

2. Don't breed a stud who has obvious congenital defects. I suggest that all studs have an X ray of the pelvis to determine the absence of hip dysplasia.

3. A stud should be used only if in excellent health and a good example of the standards of perfection of the breed. Although no dog is perfect, we should strive for perfection.

4. I would not breed any male showing emotional instability, such as timidity, aggressiveness, or viciousness.

5. Too frequent breeding, or not enough breeding, interferes with effectiveness of fertility.

6. If the male is not a proven stud, a sperm count is valuable in determining his fertility.

7. Studs that are used frequently for breeding should be on high-protein diets, such as plenty of steaks and dozens of oysters.

BREEDING CHART

1. Premating
   a. physical examination by veterinarian.
   b. laboratory examination of stools, blood, and urine.
   c. booster vaccination for distemper, hepatitis, and leptospirosis.
   d. general mating information, e.g., signs of ovulation and other pertinent information; vaginal smear (if indicated).
   e. vaginal palpation for obstructions or tumors. The veterinarian looks for anything that would interfere with penetration; if a narrow or constricted vagina, he dilates it.

2. 3-4 Weeks Postmating
   a. physical examination.
   b. dietary information and supplements.
   c. pregnancy palpation.

3. 2 Weeks Prewhelping
   a. physical examination.
   b. whelping information.
   c. clipping hair on certain breeds.

4. Postwhelping Examination Within 24 Hours After Whelping
   a. bitch: palpation for retained puppies.
   b. discharge examination and douching if indicated.
   c. injections if needed to expel afterbirth.
   d. puppies: examination for congenital defects and pediatric information to owner.

3 PRENATAL CARE

After the mating process has been accomplished, the chief concern of the breeder should be the brood bitch and the need to maintain her at optimum nutritional and muscular level. Under such conditions she can be expected to produce healthy offspring. In the bitch, successful production of healthy puppies depends on (1) fertility, (2) fecundity, (3) the ability to carry her young the full term, (4) a successful whelping, and (5) normal development of the nursing instinct and sufficient milk to nurse her puppies.

SIGNS OF PREGNANCY

1. Increase in body weight. Usually an increase in abdominal fat occurs after the 5th week of pregnancy.

2. Abdominal enlargement. Usually this is observed about the 5th week as a slight filling out of the flanks, but if the bitch is carrying a small litter, the enlargement may go unobserved. Abdominal enlargement can also be due to an infection of the uterus, or to tumors in the uterus or elsewhere in the abdominal cavity.

3. Changes in the mammary glands. Usually about the 35th day of pregnancy the teats begin to enlarge and pinken. They continue to enlarge and become softer in texture until about the 50th day. The breasts begin to fill with milk and get larger each day. A few days before whelping the breasts secrete a watery solution. The milk usually does not come down until whelping, although some brood bitches express milk several days before parturition.

A non-pregnant maiden bitch will have an enlargement of the mammary tissue after her first heat period. This is normal, and there is no need to become upset and believe that the virgin has cheated and become pregnant in an illicit romance.

4. Abdominal movement. During the last week of pregnancy, when the bitch is in a relaxed position the unborn puppies can usually be seen moving in the uterus, changing positions.

5. Temperamental deviation. During pregnancy a bitch may change in her behavior habits. Usually she becomes quieter and more affectionate, although a very nervous bitch may become aggressive.

6. There is generally an increase in appetite. But within a few days of whelping the bitch goes off her feed. When the bitch altogether refuses food, whelping is imminent. When she stops eating, and then does not deliver within 24 hours, it is a signal for a veterinarian to take over and find out what is causing the abnormality.

If none of the above signs of pregnancy are observed, there are methods that can be used by the veterinarian to determine if the bitch is pregnant. A reliable diagnosis is abdominal palpation—feeling the puppies in the uterus. Between the 24th and 30th days it is possible to feel the fetuses in the womb. With a fat bitch or a nervous one, palpation is more difficult. If only one fetus is present and is carried high in the uterus, it is difficult to make a definite diagnosis, as the puppy is under the rib cage and cannot be felt. In extremely difficult diagnosis, X ray is usually resorted to, but an X ray will not show a puppy until after the 49th day. It is not possible to use biological tests with rabbits or mice as in humans.

FALSE PREGNANCY

This is a common problem in dogs. To all intents and purposes the animal believes that she is pregnant and shows many of the symptoms of pregnancy, such as enlarged mammary glands with the production of milk, swelling of the abdomen, and appetite change. At whelping time she shows extreme hyperexcitability, such as panting and trembling. Many of these bitches go through labor pains at about the time they normally would be delivering. Often the bitch makes a nest and proceeds to protect her "puppies," which may be toys, bones, or other objects which she carries around in her mouth. She usually curls up with her "puppies" tightly snuggled to her breasts. Bitches in false pregnancy have been known to adopt entire litters of real puppies and to produce enough milk to raise them during their entire 6 weeks of suckling.

Varying symptoms are restlessness, looking for puppies, whining and crying, and scratching at rugs, trying to make a bed for her "litter." These are extreme symptoms. The dog generally doesn't go through all these antics but instead may become quiet, go off her feed, and curl up in a corner, wanting to be alone.

Certainly the behavior is abnormal for a non-pregnant dog, and while a bitch is undergoing this condition her temperament may be adversely affected. Mannerisms and normal behavior patterns are changed. Fortunately, with cessation of the false pregnancy, the bitch returns to her normal self.

Some dogs show a strong maternal impulse. In some bitches false pregnancy makes them more affectionate with their human companions, and sometimes they will mother a young puppy, or a young animal of any species. Their maternal frustrations can drive them to many things, and there are cases of bitches' stealing puppies from other bitches. Some bitches produce so much milk that it drips, stimulated by the highly emotional state. I don't advise milking such a bitch, as it will just stimulate further milk production. However, if her breasts are extremely swollen and feverish, some milk should be expressed to give relief. I would then apply camphorated oil gently to the breasts to help relieve the inflammation and dry up the milk.

The signs of false pregnancy usually last from about the 5th week following the termination of the heat period until the normal delivery date, had she been bred. Milk production sometimes lasts 4 to 6 weeks after the onset of the false whelping.

False pregnancy has been widely discussed. It is caused by retention of a growth on the ovary. The retention affects the bitch both physically and emotionally, and the abnormal behavior seems to be controlled by the ovaries that have gone astray.

Researchers have reported that an injection of certain hormones at the end of the normal heat period can prevent this condition in the ovaries and consequently false pregnancy. In treatment of false pregnancy the veterinarian usually resorts to a variety of hormones to counteract retention of the growth on the ovary.

Many times during false pregnancy the animal becomes feverish either because of enlarged breasts full of milk or because of conditions in her uterus (there are definite uterine changes during this period). A veterinarian will usually prescribe tranquilizers, and if fever is present, put the animal on antibiotics. The animal is definitely in distress both physically and mentally and needs help in both respects.

If the condition is chronic, I would advise hysterectomy to keep the animal from undue suffering. Most bitches with histories of irregular heat cycles and false pregnancies usually will not conceive when bred. However, I advise attempting to breed such a bitch, because sometimes this will cure the occurrence of false pregnancy. It has been proved that bitches who have false pregnancies are not diseased and actually when bred make excellent brood bitches.

In the maiden bitch the symptoms are usually less severe and less prolonged than in an older dog. I personally advise breeding the bitch on the next heat period, as this is one way of satisfying her maternal instincts and returning her body to that of a normally functioning brood bitch. If the owner doesn't want to raise puppies, the bitch should be spayed. Bitches who have repeated false pregnancies are prone to female infections, such as metritis and mammary tumors due to excessive lactation development.

If hysterectomy is resorted to, it is not wise to spay these dogs while they are undergoing false pregnancy, as all their female organs are swollen and hemorrhagic and the operation is difficult for them. Also, while they are lactating, an operation might prolong the production of milk from several weeks to several months. It is much wiser to wait until the bitch has completely recovered from her false pregnancy.

In the treatment of false pregnancy it is best to reduce the diet and especially the fluid intake. The more fluid the bitch drinks, the more milk she will produce. Try to feed her food as dry as possible and give her plenty of exercise to keep her bowels moving so as to excrete all the excess fluid produced by her body.

I advise keeping the bitch away from other dogs, and especially nursing bitches and young puppies. It is difficult to tell how she will react; she might jump on a nursing mother and attempt to kill her so that she can have her puppies.

False pregnancy is not to be considered a neurotic tendency, but should be considered normal behavior due to an abnormality of the ovaries. It is also incorrect to consider a bitch sexually abnormal if she undergoes a false pregnancy. Actually her maternal instincts are great, and she should make a good brood bitch.

If a bitch has a false pregnancy and then is bred and produces puppies, it does not mean that this will prevent her from having false pregnancies again. She can have further false pregnancies, although it is the experience of most breeders that if this happens, they are usually less severe and don't last as long as in unmated bitches.

PHANTOM PREGNANCY

Many a fetus dies within a day or two after mating so that there is no indication of conception, or fetuses may die and disappear several weeks after conception. Often the bitch will show all the signs of being in whelp up to the end of 6 weeks and then gradually become slimmer until she passes her whelping date without any indication of puppies.

Phantom pregnancy is entirely different from false pregnancy. It is seen in a bitch who has been mated and appears to have become pregnant with all the symptoms. Failure to whelp is usually due to the death of the fetuses in the uterus and absorption of the fetuses during some part of the gestation period. There is no secretion or discharge from the vagina to signify a miscarriage—all residue is absorbed by the body of the bitch. Sometimes a bitch will lose part of her litter, some of the fetuses will die, and she will have fewer puppies than were conceived.

Fetal death and absorption is due to some lethal factor not completely understood at this time. It is thought to be either a hormonal imbalance or a deficiency of vitamin E or a lack of certain ingredients in the maternal blood.

Having a phantom pregnancy does not mean that the bitch is sterile and unable to bear future litters.

ABORTION

There is a condition called canine brucellosis which is on the increase throughout the world. It causes abortions in affected bitches, without any warning signals, in the 40th to 50th day of gestation; the 50th day is the most common. Some of the aborted puppies don't have developed hair, and others show a swelling around the umbilical area.

Bitches who have aborted should be isolated and the contaminated area thoroughly disinfected. The affected dogs are treated with antibiotics but should not be used for further breeding until completely negative for the bacteria. Exposed males should be examined and isolated if infected, and also treated with antibiotics. The disease infrequently affects humans.

It is most commonly found in beagles and occurs in a few other breeds. After the female has aborted, there is a prolonged vaginal discharge. Diagnosis is made by a blood test or by a smear from the vaginal tract. Laboratory confirmation is the only way of knowing if the disease has affected the bitch. Any apparently healthy bitch who aborts about 20 days before her term, or who fails to conceive after 2 or 3 matings, should be suspected of having this disease.

GESTATION

We should know at the earliest possible time that a bitch is pregnant so that suitable arrangements can be made for her prenatal care.

The gestation period in normal bitches varies between 58 and 66 days; the average is 63. It varies in different breeds, and also fluctuates with the size of the litter, the time of mating, the breeding season, and environmental conditions. The smaller breeds whelp slightly earlier than the larger ones. Gestation periods have been reported from 53 to 71 days, although these should be considered unusual. Puppies born under 58 days are considered premature.

In determining the whelping date, always count from the first mating period even if there were subsequent matings. The supposition is that the bitch conceived at the first mating.

NUTRITION

Prenatal nutrition should be complete and balanced because obviously nutrition of the bitch influences the nutrition obtained by the developing puppies. If certain elements of nutrition are not supplied by the mother, the embryos will not develop normally. The bitch must have optimum nutrition for production of superior puppies.

A balanced diet should contain high-protein foods rather than dry, bulky and mushy types. Instead of giving only dry commercial food mixed with water or milk, I would supplement it with a good amount of meat, either raw or as a canned dog-food meat. High-protein foods, such as eggs, liver, milk and cheese, are also good.

When she is first bred, the bitch should not be fed too much (rationalizing that the new puppies immediately need food), or she will get fat and lazy. And during the first 4 weeks of pregnancy her food intake should not be increased. Quality food, not quantity, is what she needs.

After 4 weeks of pregnancy she should have about a 20 percent increase in food intake, while at the same time not giving her all she asks for. The increase should be in proteins rather than in starch or carbohydrates. A bitch should be in good muscular condition with no excess fat added during her gestation period.

I advise dividing the daily ration into 2 or 3 feedings, because if the bitch eats too much at one meal, it will cause discomfort from the pressure on her already overcrowded abdominal contents.

Mineral Requirements

Bone formation of puppies is largely dependent on the mineral consumption in the pregnant bitch's diet. The absorption of minerals from the diet depends on the vitamin A and vitamin D content of the diet. If the diet is deficient in these vitamins, the bitch's body will be the first to suffer from lack of minerals even though the puppies may seem normal.

If the diet is deficient in calcium and phosphorus, the bone structure of the puppies at birth may be soft, brittle, or malformed, and there will be defective teeth later in life. Rickets is a common result of mineral deficiency.

Birth defects often appear when the diet is deficient in copper, niacine, iodine, pantothenic acid, and riboflavin. Such defects include cleft palate, eye defects, and skeletal malformation.

If there is a deficiency of vitamin B_2 (riboflavin) in the bitch's diet, the puppies may be born with umbilical hernia, cleft palate, or congenital heart defects.

The last 2 weeks of gestation the puppies put on flesh, and there is little bone growth. They don't need many extra nutrients. Keep the bitch down in weight the last 2 weeks. Rearrange her diet so that she gets more animal protein and less starch and carbohydrates. And keep up the vitamins and minerals.

There is a belief that feeding the bitch supplementary vitamins and minerals while she is in whelp will produce abnormally large puppies at birth. This is a fallacy. Although inadequate nutrition in the bitch will produce weak and small puppies, the size of puppies in the prenatal stage is controlled by genetic factors and by growth hormones of the bitch.

THE FAT BROOD BITCH

Fatness in the brood bitch reduces the chances of conception and also reduces the chances of trouble-free whelping. Fat bitches often produce malformed puppies, attributable to the crowded conditions in the uterus. The brood bitch who is overweight usually has a prolonged labor process, and the puppy mortality is high.

NUMBER OF PUPPIES

Gain in body weight during pregnancy does not reflect the number of puppies in the litter.

Some people are so anxious to know how many puppies will be born that they cause the bitch undue anxiety by poking at her tummy, trying to feel the puppies. Patience is indicated.

It is possible, after the 6th week of gestation, for the veterinarian to determine the number of puppies to be born. This is done by X ray, but it is not advisable unless, for the health of the bitch, there is a need to know.

Some people think they can tell the number of puppies by counting the nipples, and the breasts that are filled with milk, believing that there will be one nipple for each puppy. This has no scientific basis.

VACCINATION

All pregnant bitches must have immunity against distemper, hepatitis, and leptospirosis. Although it is a requisite of breeding to give a bitch a booster before she is bred, it is possible for the bitch to have a booster vaccination of a modified live-virus vaccine after breeding without danger to the unborn puppies.

The importance of the booster vaccine cannot be emphasized too strongly. The mother's colostrum (first milk) obtains immunity against the various diseases puppies are prone to and should be as full of immunity as possible. Unvaccinated bitches with extremely low immunity can seriously affect the chances of puppies' surviving should they be exposed.

PARASITES

The same factors as above apply to worming. If possible, it should be done before the bitch is bred or very early in pregnancy. *A bitch should not be wormed during the last 6 weeks of pregnancy.* Worming is dangerous and can prove extremely toxic to the developing puppies. If it is necessary, be sure to see a veterinarian; he has some types of worm medicine which can be used safely on pregnant bitches. Commercial worm medicines can cause abortion or interfere with development of the embryos.

PREPARING THE BITCH FOR WHELPING

A few days before whelping it is advisable to give a bitch a good bath to be sure she is rid of external parasites, such as fleas, lice, and ticks. She should also be free of any skin diseases, such as mange, ringworm, or fungus infections, which might be transmitted to the puppies.

In the week before whelping it is advisable to clean the bitch's teeth and gums every other day. This procedure reduces the chance of navel infection in the newborn puppies. I advise using on the teeth and gums either hydrogen peroxide or salt and soda (1 tsp. of each in a cup of water).

Clip the hair around the bitch's breasts and vagina fairly short so the puppies won't become entangled during whelping and so the excess hair around the nipples will not get in the way of the hungry puppies. The inner thighs on each side of the vagina should also be clipped.

After clipping, the bitch's udder should be washed with a mild soap to cleanse it thoroughly and to wash away all parasite eggs that might be around the nipples. The nipples should be softened with baby oil and any encrustment removed. If there is dirt present on the breasts, roundworm eggs that infest so many puppies may be present. They are usually obtained by puppies in this way.

ADDITIONAL ADVICE

Bear in mind that a pregnant bitch needs special consideration in time, affection, and tender loving care. She wants to be spoiled a little bit, and I for one would be the first to give in to her demands except for extra amounts of food and in-between snacks that might cause a hazardous overweight problem. She wants to be close to you as the whelping date approaches, and she looks to you to give her the physical and emotional comfort that she will need during this especially trying time—especially the maiden bitch with her first litter.

During the last week of gestation the bitch must be watched carefully so that she doesn't injure herself and overdo herself trying to keep up with her daily chores and play periods with the neighborhood dogs. I would not allow her to roam free, as she might not be able to resist a leap or two. I would not allow her to jump over large objects; this can cause a misplacement or wrong positioning of the puppies. Or a hard fall might injure the unborn puppies. If she must be picked up, she should not be picked up in the middle but by placing one hand between her front legs and one under her hind quarters. Never, never pick up a dog by the scruff of the neck when she is heavy with pups—and I'm not in favor of picking her up in this manner even when she is not pregnant.

Normal exercise is desirable to maintain the tone of the muscles and to keep the bowels functioning normally. But the bitch should not be taken for many car rides, as hitting bumps may cause premature labor pains.

During pregnancy the bitch should be given a dose of milk of magnesia once a week to ensure regular bowel movements. I also advise a teaspoonful of bicarbonate of soda in her drinking water every day during the last half of her gestation period; this will help keep excessive acidity out of her system.

PREPARING THE WHELPING PEN

Get the whelping quarters ready for the bitch during the last week or 10 days before she is due to whelp so that she will know where you desire her to have her puppies and so she can become accustomed to it. Of course, some bitches will have their minds made up and will have a favorite bed or closet chosen where they know they will feel relaxed and be free from outside interference. However, the bitch, should be somewhere near you when she starts going into labor.

The whelping box should be in a quiet corner, free from noises, from strangers, from excitement, and from cats and other dogs in the household. If disturbed, the bitch is apt to jump up to protect her puppies and possibly hurt one of them.

The box should be about double the size of the bitch so that she can stretch out with her brood and not be in cramped quarters and liable to roll over on a puppy or step on it. For large breeds have a shelf around the bottom of the box so the puppies can crawl under the shelf and be protected from a large brood bitch.

The box should be free of any debris and in a sanitary condition. It should be scrubbed with a good disinfectant, such as Clorox or Lysol.

For the litter in the whelping box there is no substitute for shredded newspapers. Many puppies have died of strangulation from becoming entangled in blankets or towels. Cushions can also be dangerous because the bitch usually will tear them to shreds and the puppies are liable to ingest some of the stuffing. Wood shavings and straw are strictly taboo in a whelping box; the puppies may ingest or inhale particles, which would be fatal. Newspapers are easy to clean and readily available, and the price is right. The newspaper is highly absorbent, provides a good footing for young puppies and allows the bitch an opportunity to dig and scratch preceding labor. The digging and scratching reverts to ancestral days when the bitch would dig a hole in the ground for her whelping nest. Domestication has provided newspapers for the same primitive satisfactions.

The new indoor-outdoor carpeting makes ideal lining for whelping boxes. The carpeting gives the puppies good traction and is easily sponged clean. Several layers of newspapers folded under the carpet will absorb all the puddles, leaving the carpet dry.

A heating pad is a useful object to have around in case of cold puppies. It has been estimated that 50 percent of early puppy losses are due to chilling. Therefore the whelping box should be indoors, in the home, at regular room temperature, 70-72 degrees; or if it is out in the kennel, it should be provided with adequate heat and be free from drafts.

THINGS TO HAVE ON HAND FOR WHELPING

There should be a good supply of clean newspapers; delivery tends to get a little messy.

You will need towels for drying the puppies and also for grasping them in helping the bitch to deliver.

By all means don't start boiling water at the first sign of labor. Even though this is always done in the movies and on television programs, the bitch doesn't need boiling water at any time. Hot soapy water is sufficient for sanitary purposes.

You will also need a sharp pair of scissors and sewing thread or dental floss for cutting and tying off umbilical cords. Boric acid powder, BFI, or alum powder should be used on the cord when it is tied off.

You should also have a medicine dropper in case it is necessary to suck out fluid from the nostrils and mouth of a puppy.

You might have a bottle of brandy close by for the bitch, possibly for the puppies, and especially for yourself should you feel a fainting spell coming on.

4 WHELPING

No two bitches whelp in the same manner. Each bitch has her own idiosyncrasies which have to be dealt with individually. Close association between dog owner and bitch is of great help in interpreting the bitch's emotional and physical feelings as she prepares herself for the whelping process. Although it takes constant watchfulness and understanding, I should say that over-indulgence is sometimes much worse than neglect. It is upsetting to the bitch to be under constant inquisition—with a thermometer in her rectum every half hour or so and pokes and jabs at her tummy. All she wants is peace and the comfort of your presence.

Each bitch varies in emotions according to her psychological outlook, and each bitch usually goes through the same patterns each time she whelps. There are some bitches who would have their puppies in Times Square without any help in their whelping, and there are many bitches who are much more relaxed when left alone in the security and consolation of familiar surroundings. The timid, hugh-strung, or nervous dog should be kept under constant surveillance to be sure that she will go through all the normal instincts, including the care of her puppies when they are born. Some bitches will allow the owner to do almost all the whelping chores, such as cleaning the puppies and tying the cord; others will shy away and have nothing to do with the puppies if the owner interferes. You must know how the bitch will react to help or interference. The only way to know is to understand the bitch. (The central theme of this book is getting to know *your* dog.)

Although whelping is a critical time in a bitch's life, there is no immediate emergency during the whelping process that the owner should get panicky over. There will always be time to consult a veterinarian and get the bitch to the hospital if it should be required. Panic in the owner will produce panic in the dog, with possible loss of puppies and even of the bitch herself. Nature will take care of most of the situations that arise, and nature should not be interfered with but just helped along. Most bitches are capable of handling ninety-nine out of a hundred situations with their natural and maternal instincts, and the owner should not interfere with these God-given talents. The purpose of this chapter is to prepare the uninitiated to cope with the normal processes of birth and to alert them to abnormal situations so that they will know when to consult their veterinarians.

GESTATION

Although the "normal" gestation period is 63 days, there is no definite day for whelping. Puppies can be born as early as 58 days from the time of conception and survive, although they are usually a little more difficult to raise for a week or so while they catch up with their older litter mates. If they are born prior to 58 days, they usually will not survive; they are too premature, without all their body functions normal. There are reported cases of puppies born at 53 days and surviving, but such puppies require a great deal of artificial care, and probably would be lacking in normal functions.

There is no cause for anxiety or alarm unless the bitch is 4 to 5 days late. The bitch can go 65 to 68 days with normal puppies being born. However, at the 65th day the bitch should be examined by a veterinarian. If she is eating normally, seems lively, and has no off-color vaginal discharge, such as black, brown, or green, there is likely nothing to worry about.

Any normal delay in whelping, as long as 24 hours, is not endangering the puppies, because they are still enclosed in their sacs, which nourish and maintain them.

WHELPING SIGNS

One of the most reliable signs is a drop in the dam's temperature a few days before she is due. Her normal temperature is 100-102 degrees, but within 24 hours of her delivery time her temperature will begin to drop. When it reaches 99, the puppies will be born within 24 hours.

As another sign that whelping is close, the bitch lies on her side for about 12 hours. Her uterus during this period is contracting, getting the puppies into position for birth.

At this time there is usually a clear-colored discharge from the vagina. A clear discharge signifies a normal delivery. If the discharge is black, green, or brown, a veterinarian should be called immediately; something is going wrong with the delivery.

Usually about 12 hours before the puppies are born, the bitch will begin to refuse food. This is not a positive sign, because some bitches will eat right up to labor.

At about the same time she will start tearing newspapers or other objects into shreds, rugs, pillows, making a nest. And at this point she will probably go into her whelping box.

Within a few hours of delivery time the bitch will begin panting excessively, in a steady rhythm which increases as birth becomes imminent. She should be watched closely; this is a critical time. Her body will contract for a minute or so and then relax with less time between contractions as she reaches whelping. The contractions push the puppy along the uterus toward the outside world. In actual labor the uterus contracts and dilates as the puppies get into position for each stage of delivery.

NORMAL WHELPING

The first object to appear from the vagina is the water bag—the sac around the puppy which acts as a cushion to protect it from shock or injury while it is in the uterus. It also serves to dilate the vaginal passageway as the puppy moves down and out into the world.

Usually the head is the first part of the puppy to emerge, although in a normal delivery the tail or hind legs emerge first almost as often as the head. If the head comes through first, the body usually follows easily and quickly, and generally little or no assistance is required of the owner. Difficult delivery positions of puppies and how to assist are discussed in a following section.

Generally the sac surrounding the puppy bursts, or it is ruptured by the bitch as the puppy is born. Normally the bitch will instinctively tear it away with her teeth, but if she has no inclination to do so within 30 seconds after delivery, I would then interfere—as described in the next section—since the puppy cannot breathe until the membranes are torn away.

After the bitch removes the sac, she will bite through the umbilical cord and proceed to lick the puppy, rolling it around to dry it and to stimulate its respiration.

A bitch will clean her puppies roughly at times, washing their faces and rear ends and cleaning the umbilical cord. She should not be stopped unless she mauls the puppies. Most of the times her maternal instinct will motivate some degree of roughness as she is trying to stimulate breathing. The licking produces a stimulation to the blood circulation, and one can often watch pale white membranes pinken as a puppy starts breathing and his heart starts pumping blood through his body.

The afterbirth, which normally follows each puppy, is voided by the bitch within 15 minutes after the puppy is born. Most bitches then eat the afterbirth—long a subject of much controversy. Some breeders believe that the bitch needs the afterbirth because the hormones that it contains will give her a more personal feeling toward her puppies. Others think that the afterbirth is needed for certain nutritional hormones for her general well-being and to help stimulate milk production. Most experts agree that it does no harm to allow the bitch to eat the afterbirth, even though her health and well-being will not suffer should she not eat it. It is up to each owner whether to allow nature to take its course or to keep the afterbirths away from her.

Remember that there is one afterbirth for each puppy, and they should be counted to be sure they have all passed. Retention of the afterbirth results in uterine infection in the postnatal period which seriously affects both bitch and puppies.

After the first puppy has been delivered, the rest of the puppies should be delivered within 10-minute to 2-hour intervals. This varies among types of bitches. The fat bitch will take her time. The old bitch, past middle age, will usually be tired between puppies and will wait a long time. In general, a normal bitch should deliver her whole litter within an hour or two. However, it is not uncommon for it to take as long as 12 hours in a large litter, and in some extreme cases it make take 24 hours, depending on the age and condition of the bitch. Sometimes two puppies will be born within minutes of each other and then there will be a 2- to 3-hour interval. Over 3 hours between puppies is a sign of trouble.

When the second puppy is about to appear, remove the first puppy to another box to allow the bitch to concentrate on the next birth. The puppies might distract her, and in labor she might roll on one. Also, only leave one puppy at a time with her until all the puppies are born. During this process, when the puppies are away from her, they should be in a box which has an electric heating pad or a hot-water bottle. The temperature change is radical from inside the mother's womb to the outside world, and to ensure against chilling—the greatest cause of death among newborn puppies—the puppies must be kept warm.

After a few hours of whelping the bitch may get thirsty and want some warm milk or water. I would not give her any solid food; it might nauseate her. The milk or water should be presented to her in her whelping box. Don't make her get out of the box, as she most likely will not want to.

After the bitch has delivered her last puppy, wash her rear parts and her breasts to ensure that the puppies are not exposed to any soiled material that could upset their digestion. Then put the puppies on her breasts so that they can begin nursing.

Newborn puppies can go without feeding up to 12 hours after birth—in an emergency—but I would put them on the bitch as soon as she is cleaned up. The puppies should be carefully watched to be sure that each one is strong enough to grasp a nipple so that it can indulge itself in some of the colostrum which is such a vital part of its first few hours.

Once the contents of the uterus are expelled—both the puppies and the afterbirths—the uterus begins shrinking to its normal size within 24 hours after delivery. There is a normal bloody discharge for several days to a week after delivery. If the blood continues for more than a week, a complication is indicated and professional help should be sought.

Within 24 hours after birth, the bitch and puppies should be taken to a veterinarian for examination. He will expel any afterbirths that may be present and douche the bitch if purulent discharge is present. She may need pituitary to expel some of the contents, and it will help in "letting down" her milk. Most important of all, the veterinarian will ascertain if there are any unborn puppies left in the bitch. It is not uncommon for a bitch to tire out near the end of her labor and leave one or two puppies inside. She appears to go out of labor and goes about the business of nursing her puppies as if nothing were wrong. However, within 2 to 3 days, if not attended to, she develops an infection. The veterinarian will examine the vaginal tract for any tears in the cervix that might have been caused by a large puppy passing through or a difficult whelping. Such abrasions can result in infection and can also affect the bitch's future breeding status if not handled professionally.

HELPING IN LABOR

The Sac

Occasionally the sac will rupture inside the vaginal tract, causing a "dry birth," which makes whelping slightly more difficult. In a dry birth, to expedite delivery of the puppy, mineral oil can be injected into the vaginal canal to lubricate it, or a greased finger covered with vaseline can be inserted as far as possible.

Once the puppy is expelled, the sac must be removed almost immediately to initiate the puppy's breathing. If the bitch doesn't attempt to remove the sac within 30 seconds, the owner must step in and take over. The sac should be torn quickly from the puppy, taking it away from the mouth first and then off the head, enabling the newborn animal to breathe. It should be done with the puppy's head downward so that any fluid will run out of the nose and mouth.

Sometimes a puppy is born covered with a slimy dark-green sac instead of the normal healthy transparent one. This is a sign of some abnormal condition in the uterus and means either that the puppy has been in the uterus too long before delivery or that an infection has taken place in the uterus. Usually such a puppy is weaker, and I would consult with a veterinarian, as he might want to put that puppy on an antibiotic to counteract any possible infection. The green material should be washed off completely, including the mouth and nostrils. The puppy may have a greenish color for several days but soon will appear normal.

The Umbilical Cord

The puppy is attached from its navel inside the womb by the umbilical cord, which varies from 6 to 15 inches in length. The bitch must lick the puppy immediately and chew the cord within a few minutes if the puppy is to survive.

If the bitch doesn't chew the cord immediately, then the owner must take over and cut it with scissors, leaving 1 to 1½ inches of cord next to the puppy. The cord should be tied with thread or dental floss (dipped in alcohol first), and the tie should be a knot near the base of the cord to prevent bleeding. Boric acid powder, BFI, or alum powder should then be applied to the tip of the cord.

Some bitches with short mouths, such as the English bull or Boston terrier, sometimes have trouble severing the cord, and the owner should step in and do the job.

There is a hint that I would like to give owners in helping puppies—giving them a little extra blood. If the afterbirth is still attached to the umbilical cord, you can squeeze the afterbirth with your hand, forcing some blood down the umbilical cord into the puppy's body, before you sever the cord. This little extra blood can mean a life-death difference in a weak puppy.

Be careful not to pull on the cord, because this can cause an umbilical hernia and can injure the puppy fatally if there is a rupture of the blood vessels where the cord meets at the navel. Sometimes a bitch will be too rough with a puppy. She will pick it up, holding the umbilical cord in her mouth, and this is one of the predisposing causes of umbilical hernias. If you see this happening, take the puppy from the bitch, cut and tie the cord, and then give the puppy back to her if she is gentler with it.

Once the puppy is detached from the umbilical cord, he has to breathe and circulate his blood on his own. If the bitch doesn't immediately start to lick the puppy and stimulate its breathing, the owner must step in quickly and take over. Once the puppy is crying, a sigh of relief can be breathed; the instant between life and death has been successfully traversed.

Drying a Puppy

Dry a puppy by rubbing briskly with flannel or a soft bath towel. This substitute for the mother's tongue is a good stimulant for respiration and circulation. Once the puppy starts breathing normally, place him on a warm heating pad for 15 to 20 minutes. When his body temperature seems normal, he should be put with his mother to get some of her milk into him.

Difficult Delivery Positions

Although a breech presentation—when the hind feet come first—is considered normal, sometimes the bitch doesn't have enough power to pass the puppy through her pelvis. If the feet appear and the puppy is not expelled within 15 minutes, the owner should attempt to help.

Grasp the two feet (you may have to use a towel to grasp the slippery feet) and pull gently, as the bitch labors, in a downward rotating motion. If only one foot is present, find the other inside the vaginal tract before pulling on the puppy. Be very gentle, and don't use a jerking motion, as you might damage the puppy.

There are other positions which cause whelping difficulties. The puppy's head may be turned backwards—may be twisted—coming on the side. Sometimes puppies are born in an L-shape—coming at right angles. There is an upside-down position in which the puppy comes out on its back instead of its chest. All these difficult positions require professional help, and an immediate decision has to be made whether to attempt to pull the puppy or to save the bitch and the puppy intact with a Caesarean section.

Dry Birth

Occasionally a bitch that has had a difficult and long delivery will lose all the lubricating fluid in her vaginal tract. This will prevent the pup from slipping out during her uterine contractions. A solution for this problem would be to insert some lubricating substance such as mineral oil, vaseline, or olive oil inside the vagina. This lubrication will help release the puppy from the vaginal tract.

Other Delivery Problems

Another whelping problem is an extremely large puppy stuck in the pelvic canal. To save the puppy, it should not stay longer than an hour. Sometimes the owner can insert a finger (thoroughly scrubbed) into the vaginal tract and pull out the puppy. Gentle movements, from side to side, while pulling the puppy downward out of the vaginal tract will help some bitches during a difficult labor. Be gentle with the puppy, not only for the puppy's sake but also to keep from tearing the bitch's vaginal tract. If the owner cannot help the puppy to be delivered, then the bitch should be gotten immediately to a veterinarian. His expert fingers will deliver the puppy, or he will do a Caesarean section.

Another difficulty is two puppies entering the pelvic canal

at the same time. This difficult delivery requires professional help.

If no puppy appears within 2 hours after the preceding one, I would seek help. By no means insert any instrument into the bitch's vaginal tract. Besides mutilating the puppy, instruments can tear and puncture the mother's soft internal tissues and cause a fatal infection. A thoroughly washed and scrubbed finger, with or without rubber gloves, is the only thing that should enter the bitch's vagina.

Get any puppy out within an hour, dead or alive, because the rest of the litter has to be considered. If the bitch labors too hard and too long, she will become exhausted, and the longer the puppies remain in the uterus the smaller will be their chances for survival. Once labor begins, it is best to get the puppies out with the least procrastination.

Stillborn Puppies

Some puppies are born squirming, while others appear dead and lie still and cold. Don't give up on the still puppy. Rip off the sac and grab the puppy up (with a dry towel) with its head down and with a tight grasp on its body. Rub it vigorously. Swing it in a downward motion to propel any fluid from lungs, mouth, and nostrils. Do this several times. A medicine dropper or syringe is also useful in drawing fluid from the nostrils and mouth if necessary. If the puppy breathes with a gurgling sound, there is fluid in his nasal or respiratory passageway, and this should be cleaned out and dried so far as possible.

If the puppy is cold, immerse it in warm water for a minute or two to help stimulate circulation. Immerse it in water up to the neck while rubbing the chest cavity, giving a heart massage. Sometimes a stimulant, such as brandy, on the tongue works well.

Sometimes after a hard and long delivery a litter of puppies are depressed and need help in reviving. If tongues and gums are blue, it means that the puppies need oxygen badly; and some breeders keep a small tank of oxygen close by. The head cone is left in the box until all the puppies are pink and active.

If the puppies have mucus or fluid in the lungs, oxygen can save them.

If no oxygen is available, mouth-to-mouth resuscitation with artificial respiration should be administered. Blow hard enough to expand the lungs of the puppy—one breath every 2 seconds. It usually will be several breaths before a puppy will give any indication of respiratory commencement, and then he will likely begin gasping about every minute or half minute. Keep up the artificial respiration and mouth-to-mouth resuscitation until he begins breathing at a steady rhythm. If fluid develops in his mouth, keep swabbing it out or syringing it. I've worked as long as 30 minutes on a "dead" puppy, so don't give up easily. When the puppy seems to be breathing normally and is squirming about in a vigorous manner, give it to the mother and let her lick it and dry it with her tongue.

A stillborn puppy is usually due to lack of oxygen and too much fluid in the lungs caused by staying in the pelvic canal too long. It also occurs in a dry birth when the afterbirth has been severed.

CAESAREAN SECTION

The Caesarean operation has saved many a bitch and many offspring. When done in time, it is a fairly safe procedure in the hands of a skilled veterinary surgeon.

It is best not to have a Caesarean as a last resort—when the bitch is exhausted and just about dead. Blood poisoning is a dangerous thing and has shortened the life of many a bitch through neglect and delay in doing the Caesarean. Many breeders, knowing their bitches are going to need a Caesarean, will have the operation performed as soon as the cervix dilates and she is ready to deliver. Some breeds, because of their anatomical structure, for example English bulldog, Boston terrier, Pekingese, toy poodle, and Chihuahua, are prone to whelping difficulties, and the Caesarean section has been a boon to them.

As a rule of thumb, if there is a delay of more than 24 hours after labor has begun, a Caesarean section should be the procedure of choice. The sooner the puppies are gotten out of the bitch, the better chance she has for survival and the better will be the chances for raising live puppies.

There is no need for an owner to fear a Caesarean. Bitches are fully awake and able to nurse their puppies within 2 hours after surgery. They suffer no traumatic difficulties from their inability to deliver their puppies normally. There is a common misconception that once a dog has a Caesarean, she cannot be used again for breeding. I have performed four or five Caesareans on the same bitch, and she has maintained good health throughout.

Having a Caesarean operation does not necessarily mean that the next time the bitch whelps she will require another Caesarean. Some bitches have been known to undergo 4 or 5 Caesareans, and then have a normal whelping.

Factors determining the need for a Caesarian section:

—A bitch that has gone to the 65th day and does not go into active labor, yet still shows no signs of toxicity and does not respond to pituitary or tranquilizers.

—A bitch that exhibits obvious signs of difficult whelping (such as rupture of the placental membranes and loss of placental fluids, inability to deliver the fetus, or exhaustion after a protracted period of third-stage labor and no delivery of pups).

—A bitch with a prolapsed uterine horn still in labor.

—An older bitch with severe heart disease.

—Bitches with deformities of the pelvic canal that would impair delivery of the fetus.

In conclusion, let it be remembered that your Veterinarian will be the one to make the decision whether to do surgery or not.

CAUSES OF PUPPY DEATHS

Uterine Inertia

The commonest cause of death in puppies—and in bitches—is uterine inertia, which is lack of contraction of the uterus and inability of the bitch to expel her puppies.

The contractions, or labor pains, are reflex in action, and the reflex actions are thought to be controlled by hormones present in the bitch's body. However, the uterine activity which starts the labor process doesn't start the actual uterine contractions.

Uterine inertia is thought to be hereditary in origin, as it seems to run in some breeds. It may occur in bitches of any age, but the shy and nervous bitch is more susceptible. The nervous or excited animal liberates adrenalin into her blood stream, and adrenalin is a known inhibitor of uterine contractions. Such a bitch should have her owner present to help her feel more relaxed and to keep her from panicking. She should be in her normal housing environment and not in a new kennel or hospital. Anything alien to her can affect her labor pains.

Another cause of uterine inertia is hypocalcium—a lowered calcium level in the blood. A fat or lazy dog has a greater tendency toward uterine inertia. An emaciated or debilitated dog with hormonal deficiencies can also be affected by this condition. Although the causes are not exactly known the condition is thought to be due to a deficiency of necessary hormones at the termination of pregnancy.

The best way to prevent uterine inertia is to keep the bitch's weight down and to keep her active with plenty of exercise.

Dogs with uterine inertia seem normal in every respect and show all the preliminary signs of whelping, such as nest making, restless, and a slight discharge. But instead of their going into labor, the signs disappear and nothing happens.

If the puppies are not expelled after 24 hours, they are liable to run into bad problems. When there is no obstruction or abnormality, as determined by a veterinarian, uterine activity can be stimulated with small repeated does of pituitary, which may be continued, if necessary, every 20 to 30 minutes to maintain productive labor.

Unfortunately there has been promiscuous misuse of pituitary. It is a dangerous drug if used incorrectly. For instance, if the bitch's vagina is not fully dilated and her cervix has not opened sufficiently, an injection of pituitary to stimulate uterine contractions can be unproductive because of the closed cervix. This can result in a ruptured uterus and the death of all the puppies and of the bitch unless immediate surgery is performed to correct the rupture.

At times there is a secondary inertia (exhaustion). When the bitch has been in labor a long time, she may become tired and stop contracting. If the contractions are not resumed, the puppies will remain in the uterus, with serious complications.

Other Causes

A heavy prenatal infestation of hookworms or roundworms, can cause death. Puppies can be infected in the uterus, with the worms settling in the fetal liver and lungs.

Sometimes puppies are born with abnormalities of the heart, lungs, or other parts.

In the condition known as atresia anus, the puppy is born without an anal orifice. The puppy can be normal for a few days, and then there will be an enlargement of the abdomen due to inability to excrete waste products. In some cases surgery is possible.

Puppies are sometimes born with a constricted anal opening which causes chronic constipation. Enemas are needed, but the solution is for the veterinarian to stretch and dilate the anal muscles.

Sometimes puppies are born with a tendency for a telescoping of the bowels and twisted bowels. This is a common cause of death in puppies between 3 and 4 months of age.

NURSING

In my opinion there is no substitute for natural nursing, even though many good artificial methods have been devised. I don't believe that we can improve on nature in this respect. It has been proved time and again that puppies that have maternal feeding are usually stronger, more resistant to disease and parasites, and easier to rear than those with artificial feeding.

However, there are cases where artificial nursing is necessary, and countless thousands of puppies have been reared on artificial milk with good results. And in a large litter it is often necessary to supplement feeding if the bitch doesn't have enough milk for all the puppies, although they should be allowed to have as much natural milk as possible.

Although the suckling instinct is strong in puppies, sometimes the bitch with a first pregnancy doesn't know how to help the puppies. When they attempt to grasp her nipples, she growls at them, pushes them away, and sometimes even leaves the whelping box as they persist in their quest for milk. The puppies should be put directly at her breast; and if she protests, she should be scolded, and then sometimes she will allow the puppies to nurse once they start.

Sometimes the bitch doesn't have enough milk to feed her brood. The veterinarian can give her certain drugs, such as pituitary injections, to stimulate the formation of milk. To produce a plentiful supply the bitch should be in good health with adequate nutrition. Nursing puppies seem to stimulate further milk production.

Sometimes a bitch has nipples that are not fully formed. Instead of being erect and conical-shaped they resemble unripe raspberries, and it is difficult for a puppy to extract milk.

The nipples should be examined carefully to be sure they are opened and expelling milk properly. If a nipple is too large for the puppy, it may be necessary to massage the breast and milk it by hand so that it will not become caked and feverish.

There are puppies, such as cleft-palate puppies, who cannot suck milk from the breast. Watch the litter carefully and make sure that the small puppies are not being pushed away by the larger puppies. Often a small puppy is pushed off into a corner, and the mother may leave it alone to perish. She seems to sense that the puppy will sicken and die, and will not attempt to nurse it.

Sometimes after a difficult whelping the bitch may be so exhausted and frantic that she displays no interest in her puppies. The puppies should be put on her breasts.

Occasionally a puppy is too small or weak to grasp a nipple by himself and we must hold him up to his mother's breast for the first day or two, until he gains the strength to keep up with the rest of the litter. If he is too weak to suck, I usually hold him to the nipple and with the other hand massage the bitch's breast, squirting the milk directly into his mouth. This life-giving milk is very much needed by the newborn puppy. Of course, if the bitch doesn't have enough milk or if the puppy can't get milk on his own, it will be necessary to resort to a baby bottle or medicine dropper with a simulated formula.

Some bitches are not reliable and would even kill their puppies if left alone with them. In these cases we have found foster mothers, or we immediately start feeding artifically. We've saved many a puppy by using a foster mother who had puppies at about the same time—not more than a week earlier or later.

A puppy is dependent on his sense of smell, and the old saying that each puppy has its own breast and will not nurse on any other is entirely untrue. A hungry puppy will nurse on the first nipple that it finds, and instinctively grasps the teat in his mouth when he comes to it.

A good rule of thumb is that a healthy and well-fed puppy is quiet. He usually eats and sleeps. If a puppy is restless and crying it means that he is hungry and not getting his food, or is sick and in need of help. In either case it needs attention.

There are some brood bitches who start milk production several days to a week before the puppies are born. These bitches produce so much that milk drips from their breasts before the babies are born. Sometimes the breasts become caked, swollen and feverish before parturition. Help is needed because infection and fever will interfere with the health of the puppies to be born.

If a bitch is in good health and receives the proper nutrition, her breast glands will automatically release a flow of milk every 3 or 4 hours.

There is a common fallacy that the bitch needs to eat her afterbirth to produce good milk. The reasoning is that the hormones present in the afterbirth are a stimulant to milk production. This has not been corroborated by scientific research. Bitches who don't eat the afterbirth are found to produce good-quality milk.

LACTATION OF THE BITCH

Herewith is a summary of the stages of lactation. There is about a 6-week lactation period in which the bitch produces milk for her young.

The 1st to the 3rd day following the birth of the puppies is the most important period because that is when the colostrum is present in the milk. The colostrum gives the puppies their much needed protection against puppyhood diseases.

"Mature" milk is formed in the 2nd and 3rd weeks following parturition.

During the 4th and 5th weeks the milk becomes more concentrated.

During the 6th week the quantity of milk decreases, and it stops soon after the puppies are weaned.

The size of the bitch and the number of puppies influence the amount of milk produced. The breed itself has no effect on the composition of the milk; all breeds are equal in quality. It should be remembered that milk varies in quality with the diet and habits of the dam, and the milk flow can be affected by emotional factors. Where a happy, contented bitch produces a lot of milk, a nervous and panicky bitch will sometimes temporarily dry up when she is frightened or harassed by strangers coming to admire her newborn babies.

CANNIBALISM

The ancient canine instinct of cannibalism has to be watched out for in some bitches during whelping and for several days after. It can be precipitated by intense pain and fright (trying to save her puppies) and is found in certain breeds and in very nervous bitches.

The brachycephalic (large-headed, short-nosed) breeds—for

example, English bulldog, Boston bull—are predisposed to cannibalism. Their poor line of teeth and clumsiness in moving their mouth parts can bring about mutilation and even ingestion of their puppies while they are trying to sever the umbilical cord.

In the congenitally deaf breeds—for example, Dalmatian—there may also be trouble chewing the umbilical cord. Because the bitch cannot hear a puppy squealing in pain, she can mutilate it without realizing it. She should also be watched while she is tending to her puppies and carrying them around in her mouth because she may be hurting them and mutilating them without knowing it.

During a difficult whelping—trying to deliver a stuck puppy —bitches have been known to mutilate and eat the puppy while pulling at it to remove it from the vagina.

Certainly if a bitch shows any viciousness toward her puppies, they should be kept apart from her. If they are nursed by her, it should be done only while the owner is in close attendance.

A nervous bitch should be closely watched and all fear-provoking factors, such as noises, strangers, and too much handling of the puppies, should be kept from her.

There is a theory that cannibalism is linked to lack of certain hormones and that ingestion of the puppies satisfies the deficiency. There is no supportive conclusive evidence for this theory.

5 POSTNATAL CARE OF THE BITCH AND PUPPIES

THE BITCH

After the initial critical whelping period is over, the normal bitch settles down in her nest with her puppies and should require little care. If she is in good health and has an adequate diet with the proper supplements, she should produce enough milk to keep her puppies content and healthy.

It is best to avoid handling the puppies for the first 10 days or so, except when absolutely necessary. Some bitches resent their brood's being handled by anyone but themselves and will lick their puppies thoroughly after the owner has put them back in the box, trying to erase fingerprints and scent.

After the bitch has completed her whelping process, she is exhausted and relieved. I would attempt to clean her breasts with a wet cloth, and her rear legs and vagina to remove any debris for the puppies to ingest. I would change the papers in her whelping box and give her some milk or broth to drink.

The Milk

The normal mother should then settle down and tend to her puppies and nurse them. Her maternal instincts should take over; a good brood bitch will lick her puppies, clean them and dry them, and produce milk for her newborn family.

Colostrum, the first milk secreted by the mammary glands, is created for only the first 6 to 12 hours after birth and possesses anti-bodies that give the puppies resistance to diseases. The nursing puppy who gets colostrum gets good early protection for a long time. Any failure in nursing colostrum lowers a puppy's resistance to disease and other environmental factors that come along. If for some reason a puppy does not receive colostrum, I advise injections of canine globulin to protect him against the ravages of puppyhood diseases.

Milk production in the bitch is largely controlled by hormones, as is the maternal instinct. An inadequate milk supply or unwillingness to nurse is usually due to a lack of these hormones that are formed at whelping time. Some bitches are stimulated in their milk production by injections of hormones, such as pituitary.

On the other hand, lactation is stimulated by suckling. The milk flow is usually adjusted to the demands of the puppies, and many a bitch has nursed 12 to 13 puppies without outside help. This is a tremendous drain on the bitch's body, and her diet has to be supplemented with all the calories, vitamins, and minerals necessary to feed the extra little creatures.

The Problem Bitch in Nursing

Sometimes the maternal instinct doesn't take over, and the bitch is indifferent to her newborn litter. This indifference can be due to a background involving poor rearing, poor feeding, lack of proper exercise, or debilitation from injury or disease. Some of these bitches are products of show-dog breeding where the sole interest is in visual points without regard to fertility, litter size, ability to whelp normally, or maternal instinct. Other bitches after whelping are exhausted, hysterical, or in a state of shock from the traumatic experience of a first litter.

A bitch who shows downright aggressiveness toward her puppies should be tranquilized and the puppies removed from her until she becomes calm; otherwise she may hurt the puppies, or even kill them, or she may even devour them. When she has calmed down—and this applies to all indifferent bitches—she should be made to lie on her side and be firmly held while the puppies are put to her breast and allowed to nurse. For some bitches this will overcome the fear of the puppies, and they will then take them over. If the bitch persistently refuses to nurse her puppies, putting them to her breasts and allowing them to suckle for 15 to 20 minutes at a time is necessary for the first few days. After this time she will usually allow them to nurse by themselves.

If puppies don't nurse, the milk decreases and stops altogether within 24 hours. If for some reason the puppies are removed from a nursing bitch, or die, there has to be some help for her milk-filled breasts. Injections of hormones can help decrease the milk supply, and the breasts can be bathed with camphorated oil to help the flow decrease. The diet should be changed to a light one with little fluid and no raw red meat. The bitch should be put on laxatives to keep her bowels open and draw fluid from her body.

Foods that seem to stimulate milk production in the bitch are milk, raw meat, eggs, fish, liver, and other organ foods. A nursing bitch should be fed 4 to 6 times a day with the last feeding just before bedtime because the puppies nurse on her during the night as well as all day. Supplements of vitamins, calcium, phosphorus, and other minerals should be included in her diet. There is a tremendous drain on her blood calcium, and a deficiency will lead to eclampsia, bone deformities, faulty teeth formation, and other defects in puppies and bitch.

Nutrition During Lactation

The first week after the puppies are born, the bitch's diet should be light, consisting mainly of milk and eggs with cereal and biscuits. The bitch should not be overfed the first week, as this may cause an overproduction of milk which can lead to breast problems.

After the bitch has returned to normal and the puppies are nursing and keeping the breasts depleted, her diet should gradually be increased. She needs plenty of high-protein food, such as meat, eggs, liver, and milk. Raw meat is an excellent way of providing her with the best food for stimulating milk production, and lots of fluids should be given for the same purpose. Supplementary vitamins and minerals are of utmost importance in the bone formation of the puppies and for the bitch's well-being.

The vital time for nutrition during lactation is between the 2nd and 5th weeks. During this period the food intake has to be multiplied at least 3 times. For example, a cocker spaniel with a normal daily maintenance requirement of 1 pound will require 3 pounds a day for adequate lactation during the 2nd to 5th week.

The food-consumption peak is during the 5th week, and from this point on the puppies usually will have supplementary feedings and demand less and less mother's milk.

If the bitch seems to be producing too much milk, her intake of milk and other fluids, and of raw meats and protein-rich foods, should be reduced.

As the puppies are being weaned the bitch's diet should be increasingly lighter. By the end of 6 weeks she should be receiving fewer supplements and less food in order to help her drying process.

Behavior With Her Puppies

The first few days after whelping the bitch is reluctant to leave her puppies even to go outside to relieve her bowels and bladder, but for her general comfort and health she should be encouraged to do so. During the first 2 weeks she will not leave her puppies for more than a few moments at a time.

For the first 5 days after whelping the bitch should leave the box 4 or 5 times a day to relieve herself. After the 3rd day her outings should be for longer periods and by the end of the first week she should be having regular walks and exercise to keep her body functioning normally. Exercise also seems to stimulate lactation.

The bitch needs to be assured that her puppies will not be disturbed while she is away from them. The fewer people who see the puppies until after weaning, the better the dam will feel and the less exposure the puppies will have to disease. When it is necessary to let people see the puppies, always take the dam away from the whelping box so that she will not hurt the puppies or attack a stranger. And never, never let the neighbor children try to pick up her puppies.

A spoiled house pet may go off her feed for the first several days after her first litter. This is usually due to emotional factors (but I would check her temperature to see if fever is present). Such a spoiled pet may be tempted with her favorite delicacies.

Sometimes a bitch will vomit her food, and then her puppies will eat it. Although disgusting to watch, it is part of her ancestral instincts. She partially digests the food and then regurgitates it as a step between breast feeding and teaching the puppies to eat solid food. The bitch should not be punished, and I would endorse the action by letting the mother dog wean her puppies in this manner.

Postwhelping Problems

For the first week after whelping the bitch's temperature should be taken at least once a day. Any reading above 102 degrees indicates a problem. It can be due to an infection in the uterus or to a retained afterbirth. It can also be due to an inflammation of the breasts (mastitis). Constipation or diarrhea also cause fever. The constipation is easily relieved with milk of magnesia; in severe cases an enema may be indicated. I personally advise a routine dose of milk of magnesia following parturition; it helps clean out all the debris the bitch has eaten during birth. Diarrhea is debilitating, and the bitch will refuse food and even refuse to nurse her puppies. As a preventive it is advisable to restrict her diet for the first few days.

For about a week after delivery there is a vaginal discharge, usually reddish in color, and varying in quantity from a slight drip, which is normal, to a more copious discharge, which signifies some abnormality. Most bitches will keep themselves clean by licking themselves and will keep the signs of discharge from sight. However, when there is some abnormality in the vaginal tract—either an infection in the uterus due to a retained afterbirth or a tear of the cervix—the color of the discharge will vary from normal red to brownish or purulent.

When a retained afterbirth, a mummified fetus, or a dead puppy remains in the uterus, there will be a brownish color and sometimes a blackish-green discharge and the bitch will usually show signs of being feverish and lethargic, will refuse her food and will sometimes refuse to nurse her puppies. Her temperature may rise to 103-105 degrees, and she is obviously a sick dog. A veterinarian should be consulted immediately, to save not only her life but the lives of her puppies, since her milk will be affected.

If the normal red vaginal discharge continues for more than a week, it signifies some abnormality in the vaginal tract. Upon examination the veterinarian will usually find a tear in the cervix due to some problem in delivery. Those tears heal slowly and give a continuous discharge. If they are not treated properly, they can result in scar tissue which may prevent conception in subsequent breeding.

Postwhelping Complications of the Bitch

Mastitis. This is caused by the milk not being sucked by the puppies, because of either deformed nipples or an overproduction of milk. The bitch becomes restless with a high temperature and refuses to eat. The breasts are feverish and swollen, with sometimes a reddish-blue appearance.

Cold packs or hot Epsom salt applications are usually helpful in bathing the breasts, and camphorated oil will help draw out some of the inflammation.

If a breast is extremely enlarged, which usually occurs in the rear two breasts, it should be milked by hand to draw out some of the coagulated and caked milk. The mother's temperature sometimes reaches 104-105 degrees, which is usually a danger signal that an abscess is forming in the breast. A veterinarian is indicated in these cases to prevent danger to the mother and the puppies. The puppies will sometimes nurse at infected breasts, only to get the infection themselves, and this can result in death.

Eclampsia (Milk Fever). This is a condition encountered in the bitch after whelping. It is due to a lowering of the blood calcium due to exhaustion by the puppies. It is usually seen in small breeds with large litters and may occur anywhere from 1 day to 4 or 5 weeks after whelping. Occasionally it will occur prior to whelping if the bitch is very deficient in calcium and there is not enough for the developing fetuses in her uterus. To save the bitch's life, immediate treatment by a veterinarian is necessary. He will give her intravenous injections of calcium.

One of the first signs is restlessness in the bitch. Her eyes show an anxious look. Respiration is short and rapid. The mucus membranes become pale. The bitch has spasms in which her legs and body shake in a jerking motion. She may lie on her side, kicking all four feet and salivating profusely. She is subject to paralysis, collapse, foaming at the mouth, and labored breathing. Temporary relief before she reaches the veterinarian is a spot of brandy as a heart stimulant. If there is no treatment within 12 hours, she will die.

Most bitches if treated in time recover without any complications. The bitch's nursing duties should be curtailed for 2 to 3 days with no puppies nursing her (the puppies will have to be nursed by hand); then, after she is fully recovered, they can gradually be allowed to nurse for possibly half an hour at a time 2 or 3 times a day. Careful return to nursing duty is necessary because the attack can recur. The bitch should be on high doses of calcium, phosphorus, and vitamins to prevent recurrence.

Agalactia (inadequate or no milk supply). This condition can usually be detected from unthrifty puppies, hungry puppies, and overactive and crying puppies. The bitch's milk can be helped in flow by pituitary and other hormones. Increasing her diet with high-protein food and plenty of fluids will also help in milk production.

Metritis (infection of the uterus). This may occur after an extremely difficult labor, and often develops into pneumonia, which is evidenced by a rapid pulse, high temperature, drooping head, and refusal to lie down because of severe chest pains. Professional help is needed immediately to save the bitch.

Hair Loss in Lactating Bitches

Many bitches, particularly the long-haired breeds, lose much of their hair following whelping. This hair loss is usually related to diet—feeding a low-energy diet which may be adequate for the normal mature adult dog but is inadequate nutritionally for the lactating bitch. A diet ample in protein and fat may help prevent postparturition hair loss and maintain the lactating bitch in good health.

Many bitches shed a lot of hair and have a dry unsightly coat after feeding a litter of puppies. But with proper diet and worming after she is rid of her puppies, within 3 or 4 weeks the bitch will regain her girlhood beauty.

THE PUPPIES

Nursing

Watch the puppies closely for the first 48 hours to make sure that they are all nursing with strong sucking motions. Sometimes a weak or small puppy will be pushed into a corner to die, and the mother will refuse to take care of it. This puppy can be hand-fed, and he usually will catch up with his litter mates after the first week. At times there will be a tiny puppy who is too small to nurse by himself; he doesn't have the strength. He can be lifted to a nipple and some of the colostrum squirted into his mouth.

Supplementary feeding to these weak puppies should be done with either a home formula or a commercial formula, such as Borden's Esbilac. Goat's milk is strengthening to newborn puppies. When supplementary feeding is given, the puppy can be returned to the nest between feedings; the bitch will lick and clean him and keep him warm.

A weak puppy who cries constantly and appears limp and cold is in critical condition. It should immediately be removed from the litter and put in a warm box with a hot-water bottle or an electric heating pad. It should be fed every half hour with glucose or water or milk, and if necessary a drop or two of brandy for stimulation.

When a puppy refuses to nurse, or the bitch doesn't produce enough milk, it is necessary to try to teach him to nurse, and if this is impossible, he must go onto artificial feeding. Putting the puppy to the bitch's nipple and squirting milk into his mouth is a good way to start his reflexes. Usually once he tastes the warm milk he will begin to suckle and continue with pleasure.

Watch the two back breasts of the bitch, which are usually the largest and the most filled with milk. Sometimes they are too large and swollen for the puppies to nurse, and instead of being relieved, the bitch gets feverish, and an infection or an abscess occurs in the breasts. If the puppies will not nurse on the two back breasts, the breasts should be milked by hand until they are small enough for the puppies to suckle. If the litter is small, the puppies should be placed on the breasts most filled with milk. By rotating the puppies none of the breasts will get caked with excess milk production.

As determined in a recent study, one-third of breast-fed puppies are dissatisfied with mother's milk. The puppies were unduly restless and didn't thrive or grow as they should have. In such cases bottle feeding is certainly indicated for the benefit of both puppies and bitch. There are some bitches whose quality of milk and possibly even quantity is not sufficient to satisfy the growing needs of their puppies.

Care and Feeding of Orphans

There are many reasons why some puppies need individual hand feeding, and the most common occurrence is the death of the bitch. Other reasons include puppies born by Caesarean section with complications causing the bitch to be unable to nurse for the first day or two; small immature puppies too weak to suckle; the bitch's rejection of a small or weak puppy in her brood; and too large a litter.

Raising puppies by hand requires perseverance and a careful tedious technique because of the complications that can result if, for example, a puppy ingests milk too quickly or ingests too much air. There are three factors to consider in artificially raising a litter of puppies: (1) the feeding formula must simulate the bitch's milk, (2) furnishing the proper environment, and (3) furnishing proper management.

The Feeding Formula. For healthy and vigorous puppies it is necessary to simulate a formula similar in quality and quantity to mother's milk. There is a home formula which is time-proven, or there's the excellent commercially prepared formula put out by Borden—Esbilac—which meets the specific and nutritional requirements of young puppies. It is a carefully balanced blend of proteins, fats, carbohydrates, vitamins, and minerals which makes it near perfect as an alternative or supplement for bitch's milk.

The home formula is good: a can of evaporated milk, equal parts of boiled water, the yolk of an egg, a tablespoon of Karo syrup (light or dark), and a teaspoon of limewater. This can be prepared, kept refrigerated, and small amounts warmed to the correct temperature at feeding time.

There are plastic nursing bottles, either baby-doll bottles or premature-infant nipples which have anticolic nipples (usually with three holes). These prevent too much air being gulped by the puppy.

Some people feed whole goat's milk and claim excellent results.

The formula must not give indigestion or colic to the puppy, and must not produce diarrhea. If the homemade formula produces diarrhea, the Karo syrup should be eliminated, as it has some laxative qualities.

The Proper Environment. Without a doubt the most serious danger to a newborn puppy is chilling, as he has no heat-control mechanism to protect him. An incubator-type box can be fixed with either an electric heating pad or an overhead infrared bulb; or an electric bulb can be used to keep the temperature between 85 and 90 degrees for the first 5 days, at about 80 degrees for the next 2 weeks, and gradually dropping down to 70-75 degrees by the end of the 4th week. But overheating is almost as bad as chilling, and the incubator box must be well regulated. If it gets hot, the puppies will pant.

It is also advisable to separate the puppies into individual pens because in the absence of their mother's breasts they tend to suckle at each other's tails and genitals. Also, with individual compartments it is possible for the owner to check on stools and be sure there is no diarrhea or constipation. Each compartment should be lined with a clean soft diaper or folded newspaper. A diaper or towel should be pinned smoothly to the box so that the puppy cannot crawl under it and become entangled and smother.

Proper Management. Proper management of the orphan puppy is guided by his regular increases in weight and the feel of his body. If he is not receiving enough fluid through the milk, he will tend to feel hidebound or dehydrated. A puppy should be round and fat.

The condition of his stool is an important guideline. Consistency and regularity indicate health, and any derangement in the consistency of bowel movements indicates some abnormality. A normal stool should be firm and yellowish in color. A normal puppy that is fed 3 to 4 times a day should have 3 to 5 movements. A good rule of thumb is a bowel movement for each time he is fed.

Feeding the Orphan. At least 3 feedings a day at 8-hour intervals are required. Some puppies will want a 4th feeding. Most people who feed every 2 hours find this quite unnecessary unless the puppies are very weak and are recovering from an illness and need extra strength. A sick or weak puppy may have to be fed every half hour or so, a few drops at a time, for maximum strength.

Most researchers agree that demand feeding is best. When the puppy is sleeping, he should not be bothered. When he wakes and begins stirring, he should be fed.

In the amount to be fed, a rule of thumb is to feed enough so that the abdomen is somewhat enlarged after feeding. The puppy should not be given all he would eat, because this would cause his abdomen to become overextended or bloated and contribute to all sorts of digestive upsets, such as colic, indigestion, and diarrhea. It is best to underfeed for the first 2 or 3 days and then bring the puppy up to full feeding by the 4th or 5th day. By this time he should be accustomed to the formula.

After 2 to 3 weeks on the formula the puppy can be started on a high-protein instant baby cereal such as Pablum, mixed with either Esbilac or a homemade formula.

At 3 weeks the puppy can be weaned to pan feeding. A good

way is to put a finger into the soupy-type mixture and let the puppy suck the finger. Puppies have to be taught to lap, and sometimes they have to be spoon-fed for a few days because they will eat solids before they will learn to eat from a bowl or pan. At this age small amounts of canned dog meat or crumbled hamburger meat can be added to the cereal and the milk formula.

From the 3rd to the 4th week puppies can lap from their pan and eat on a regular schedule in between play and exercise.

At 4 weeks they should be completely weaned from the Esbilac or home formula and should be eating their food at the rate of 1 teaspoon per 5 pounds of body weight at each meal.

Techniques of Feeding. In feeding it is best to place the puppy on his stomach. He should never be placed on his back or the nipple or dropper inserted into his mouth while he is on his back, else he will likely inhale some of the formula, which will cause coughing and possibly a foreign-body pneumonia.

The formula should be lukewarm or tepid—with the chill taken off.

The puppy should never be fed rapidly. If ever there is milk bubbling from the puppy's nostrils, it means that the milk is being forced down his throat too fast, and he is liable to choke. Either the medicine dropper is too large or the holes in the nipple are too large, and replacement should be made.

The bottle should be held at about a 45-degree angle, and no air should be allowed to enter the puppy's mouth. Gulping air leads to indigestion.

The nipple should be tested to make sure the puppy is getting enough milk. When the bottle is held upside down, the milk should ooze slowly from the opening. If the rate of flow is not free enough, the holes can be enlarged with a red-hot needle.

After each feeding the puppy should be burped. He should be held upright against a shoulder while being rubbed and patted on the back. Burping will prevent a lot of digestive disturbances.

Urination and Defecation. For the first week of his life a young puppy relies on instinct for urination and defecation. These functions may have to be aided by the owner. To stimulate the natural acts, after each feeding the anal and abdominal regions should be gently rubbed with a cotton swab slightly moistened with warm water or baby oil.

The puppy should not be handled any more than necessary, but when his body needs have been taken care of his skin should be gently washed with warm water after each feeding and defecation.

Constipation. Constipation usually causes a swelling of the abdomen and colicky pains. A further addition of Karo syrup or honey to the formula will have a mild laxative affect. If the bowels continue sluggish, a drop or two of mineral oil on the puppy's tongue should straighten out the complication. Unless regular defecation after each meal is maintained, bowel disorders may develop that will jeopardize the puppy's chances for survival. In severe cases a warm-water soapy enema is indicated.

Diarrhea. A loose stool can mean that the puppy is ill or is being overfed, or that the formula is too rich to suit his intestinal assimilation. At the first sign of diarrhea the formula should be diluted in half by adding more water and cutting out the Karo syrup. Kaopectate is excellent to help stop the diarrhea ($\frac{1}{2}$ tsp. per 5 lb. of body weight 3 times a day). If the diarrhea persists, a veterinarian should be consulted.

Grooming. Daily grooming is a necessity and should consist in wiping the puppy's eyes with a boric acid solution and gently massaging the skin, which stimulates circulation and thoroughly awakens the puppy. The best time for massage is just before feeding, while the formula is being warmed. The best way to do it is to stroke the puppy's sides and back with a soft folded diaper. It is also good to occasionally rub the puppy's skin with baby oil because of the drying effect of the incubator heat. If absolutely necessary, puppies can even be washed in warm water and rubbed dry with a soft towel or diaper.

Feeding Equipment. All feeding equipment should be thoroughly scrubbed, as disease may result from contaminated formula or unsanitary feeding equipment. Formula should be made up in small batches, for a day at a time, and then warmed as needed. A premature-baby nipple with an ordinary baby bottle is the most desirable apparatus for feeding orphan puppies.

Canine Globulin. Research has proven that certain hand-reared puppies are especially susceptible to infection and are usually more easily infested with worms than are naturally nursed puppies. I advise giving orphan puppies canine globulin within 24 hours after birth to build up their resistance to disease. They would normally have gotten this from the colostrum of their mother.

Immersion Feeding of Puppies. An alternative to bottle or syringe feeding, this is an excellent method of feeding orphan puppies and puppies of dams that cannot rear their young. This method consists of plopping the youngsters into a shallow dish or pan containing the proper formula. Some pups begin lapping immediately while others may take several days before they catch on to the idea. The dish, with sides high enough to keep them from crawling out, must not be filled to a point where they would drown. In the beginning, they have to be watched carefully so that they do not get into the habit of taking in milk through the nose. Then they have to be wiped off after every meal until they are big enough to eat the food from outside the dish.

It is important to remember that only healthy puppies should be tried on this method and their throats should be checked before attempting this procedure. If a pup has a cleft palate or an opening in the soft palate, the milk would be aspirated into the lungs and a fatal pneumonia would result. Have your veterinarian check the soundness of the throat to avoid any serious problems.

The Tube Method of Emergency Feeding. A new method of feeding newborn puppies, particularly weak or sick puppies, has come into prominence in recent years and has been enthusiastically received. This tube method must be fully understood and performed correctly, otherwise fatalities can result. It is especially life-saving for cleft-palate puppies, as the milk doesn't get into the nasal passages but is injected directly into the stomach.

Small rubber catheters are used, attached to a large hypodermic syringe which holds between 20 and 40 cubic centimeters and may be adequate for several puppies without refilling. The feeding end of the tube is inserted into the puppy's mouth and when it has gone down to about the puppy's last rib a mark is made on the tube, at the mouth, as a guide for future feeding. The tube is attached to the syringe and the formula is injected. Not only milk supplements but diluted strained baby foods can be forced through the tube.

The tube should be inserted into the puppy's mouth without forcing it and usually the puppy will swallow the tube. If the tube is forced into the mouth, it may go into the windpipe, with dire results. Before the milk is given, a drop should be inserted and if the puppy coughs it means that the tube has gone down into the windpipe and should be withdrawn from the mouth immediately.

I advise the novice to get instructions from his veterinarian on how to insert the tube and on the techniques for feeding. The method takes skill, patience and dexterity but is well worth learning. For small breeds a No. 8 catheter is recommended and for larger breeds a No. 10.

Tail Docking, Dew-claw Removal, Nail Clipping

Tails should be docked 48 to 72 hours after birth. There is less pain sensation in the newborn puppy; after his tail is removed, he curls up and goes right back to sleep. The bleeding must be stopped before the puppy is put back in the litter.

Each breed has a requirement for tail length, and many a potential champion has been ruined because his tail was cut too short. When in doubt leave a longer tail; it can always be recut.

A veterinarian should do the surgery, since he will know the proper length and procedure. It will be shaped and tapered and give a satisfactory appearance.

There are quacks who use a tight rubber band at the desired tail length, and after about 4 days the tip "falls off." I don't recommend this method, as it often leaves a badly scarred tail tip.

Some breeds require front dew claws to be removed (French poodle, Sealyham, wire-haired terrier, Doberman). In all breeds, if the claws are found on the rear legs, they should by all means be removed, as they usually would cause trouble later in life. They perform no function, and many a dog has lost his eyesight by being scratched by a dew claw while playing. When dew claws are allowed to remain, they often interfere with a dog's running and cause trouble when they tear off.

Puppies' nails should be clipped at 2, 4, and 6 weeks of age to avoid scratching and injuring the mother's breasts. Any type of nail clipper can be used, and only the tips of the nails should be cut to avoid bleeding. If bleeding occurs, apply alum powder or a styptic pencil to the nail tips.

Fat and Lazy Puppies

This occurs occasionally when there is a litter of only one puppy. There is no competition so it usually eats and sleeps all the time. It is important to make this puppy exercise, before it is too late, i.e. not over 3 weeks of age. Otherwise the puppy will grow up with bad leg coordination.

Growth Rate in Puppies

In the growth of puppies little gain is made the 1st week, but weight is added rapidly during the 2nd week and thereafter. Weight gains in puppies from small litters are uniformly higher than in puppies from large litters—four or more. However, the rate of gain at this stage doesn't affect adult size. After the puppies are weaned and eating by themselves, if they are given the proper foods, they will usually gain their normal weight up to their breed standard. Puppies getting too little protein, or protein of a poor quality, may still grow normally but will be more susceptible to infections.

St. Bernards and other large breeds increase their weight 40 times in the first 6 months and 60 times in the first year of life.

Some researchers have come up with the theory that overfeeding growing puppies to make them big and healthy-looking may be doing them a disservice, because the faster growth frequently results in loss of longevity. These researchers have shown that the life span can be increased by delaying the maturity of the offspring.

Mortality in Newborn Puppies

The critical stage of the puppy's life is the 1st week. The causes of death during this 1st week involve various congenital defects, environmental defects, and injuries as a result of difficult whelpings, but the greatest number of puppy deaths are attributed to chilling and to an infectious disease known as canine herpes virus.

Chilling of Puppies. When the newborn puppy leaves the warmth and security of the dam's body, during the first few minutes his body temperature drops sharply.

During the first few days of life puppies have no shivering mechanism to regenerate heat loss when the room temperature is lower than the temperature of the nest. Consequently their body temperatures can drop quickly, and they develop cooling of all body functions.

When a puppy becomes cold, he seeks shelter. He tries to nuzzle against his mother's breast or cuddle with another puppy for warmth. If this is not possible, his body temperature drops quickly.

If the puppy remains cold for as long as 48 hours, he will fail to gain weight. However, once a cold puppy is put into a warm temperature, such as an incubator temperature of 85-110 degrees, there is a distinct increase in his temperature, and he will begin gaining weight. The body temperature begins at about 90-95 degrees for the 1st week and gradually increases up to the normal range of 100-102 degrees by the 5th to 6th week.

One of the first signs that a puppy is becoming chilled is restlessness and crying. As the puppy becomes colder a high-pitched note occurs with almost every respiration, and the respiratory rate increases about 30 per minute. A rectal thermometer will show a fall in temperature from 96 degrees down to about 70 degrees. The puppy will become cold to the touch, limp, pale-gummed, and appear in a state of death.

The puppy can sometimes be revived if quickly immersed in hot (not scalding) water, and rubbed and stimulated.

Canine Herpes Virus ("Fading Puppy Syndrome"). This is an insidious disease because the bitch appears healthy, the milk production seems adequate, and all the puppies nurse in a normal manner until just a few hours prior to their deaths.

The early signs of the disease are sudden cessation of nursing, chilling, and painful crying. Abdominal pain is a diagnostic feature which is nearly synonomous with a yellowish-green diarrhea. The cry of the puppy is pitiful (one of screaming agony) since the abdominal contents are in profuse spasms. The yellowish-green stool usually appears 3 to 4 hours before death, and then the acute abdominal pain begins, and sometimes retching and vomiting is seen. The puppies stop nursing when the crying begins, their breathing becomes labored, and they begin to gasp shortly before death. It usually affects puppies about 1 week after birth, and the puppies continue to die over a 2-week period until all the puppies in the litter are dead.

I would attempt to have the puppies treated, although success is not encouraging. Vitamin K injections are given to help prevent internal hemorrhaging. Blood building vitamins are given to the puppies by mouth, and in a sick puppy blood transfusions are used to try to build up resistance to the infection. The puppy has to be force-fed by dropper because usually he will refuse to eat.

It is believed that puppies acquire the infection while passing through the vagina during the whelping process. It is thought to be present in the vagina and not in the uterus. The herpes virus is not in any way related to canine distemper or canine hepatitis. Usually puppies older than 3 weeks will not die but go through mild symptoms of the infection. Most deaths occur up to 14 days after birth. Post-mortem examination shows areas of hemorrhage in liver, lungs, and kidneys. At present there is no vaccine for the prevention of the disease.

Adult dogs sometimes show the disease in a mild way and recovery is uneventful, even though it is 100 per cent fatal in puppies under 2 weeks of age. The sire has not been found to transmit this disease from bitch to bitch, and if a bitch loses a litter it does not necessarily mean that she ever will again. In fact, many bitches have produced normal healthy litters the following year. However, the bitch may be a carrier and lose the litter each time she whelps. The infection may be spread from infected bitches to other bitches through either vaginal or throat secretions and is spread by direct contact between susceptible dogs. But the stud is not an intermediate carrier.

There are various theories regarding the prevention of the disease. Some breeders feel that the absence of vitamin K in dogs enables the virus to predominate. Alfalfa is the only cereal known to contain vitamin K. Wheat-germ cereal or oil is also advisable (to be given to bitches prenatally). If the bitch shows signs of a vaginal infection, by a vaginal discharge, within 2 weeks of whelping, douching with an antiseptic solution should be done at least twice a day to try to clear up the infection before the puppies arrive.

Some breeders advise the use of gamma globulin in suspected cases—given to bitches within a week before they whelp and to the puppies soon after birth to help prevent the virus infection from getting started. Gamma globulin doesn't affect an already established infection but might help prevent one from getting started. Antibiotics, such as terramycin and chloromycetin, can be used but are not especially beneficial in fighting the virus. They do help secondary infections.

Although no vaccine is available for herpes virus at present, hopefully there will be one in the near future. Some bitches who have natural immunity may transfer this immunity to their puppies through the colostrum. Maiden bitches with the first litter can usually be expected to be exposed to this virus, transmitting it to their litters.

Puppy Strangles (Mumps). Caused by staphylococci, this disease usually develops when the puppy is 4-5 weeks of age. The puppy develops a skin condition around the muzzle. It spreads to the eyes and ears and then the gland under the neck begins to swell and the puppy looks as if it has the mumps. Treatment is successful if started early.

Blood Poisoning. A bacterial infection in a dogs bloodstream, this infection can occur at 4-40 days of age and is usually derived from the bitch or the environment. The usual symptoms are crying and straining and the puppy begins to become bloated. Usually within 18 hours the puppy is dead.

The puppies should be taken from the bitch until the infection is cured, without care entire litters of puppies are lost. If the puppy does live he is likely to have kidney damage.

The only cure is preventive medicine. Always examine the bitches vulva and the stud before breeding. A blister that resembles a cold sore may be carrying the virus which will affect the vaginal tract at the time of whelping. A human douche solution may be used on the bitch just prior to whelping.

Other Causes of Death in Puppies. There are congenital defects in puppies affecting the digestive, respiratory, and circulatory systems. Heart defects in young puppies have been shown to exist much as in human babies. If a puppy dies from a congenital defect, we must recognize it and avoid use of the breeding stock that is producing it.

There is also a congenital abnormality in the lung tissue which results in respiratory failure before death. Sometimes this abnormality can be traced to a partial failure of the lung tissue in the bitch's womb. The defect results in fetal fluid in the lungs, which brings about the early death of the puppy because of his failure to breathe properly. Such a puppy is usually born alive but dies during the first few days of life. He refuses to eat, becomes dehydrated and soon gives up the struggle for life. If it is a congenital abnormality of the lungs, no treatment is possible, but if it is caused by an infection, the veterinarian, with the use of antibiotics, can possibly control the loss.

Signs of a Sick Puppy

It is critically imperative to spot a puppy in the early stages of any sickness because an hour, even minutes, can mean the difference between life and death. Some signs of sickness are:

1. Rejection by the dam. Instinct seems to tell the bitch when a puppy is sick, and she will usually push it aside to die. However, if such a puppy is discovered in time, it can possibly be saved.

2. Cessation of nursing. Whenever a puppy doesn't nurse, it means that there is trouble. If it is merely a matter of needing to be taught, this should be done, or the puppy should be reared by hand.

3. Crying. It is necessary to differentiate between a hungry puppy and a sick puppy. In either case help is needed. A quiet, sleeping puppy is a healthy one.

4. Weakness or limpness. It is easy to spot a vigorous, healthy puppy by its quick movements. In contrast a sickly puppy moves slowly and with a lot of effort.

5. Dehydration. Normally the skin of a puppy is resilient. If upon lifting the skin it doesn't bounce back into place, it indicates that the puppy's body is beng depleted of fluids. This can mean lack of sufficient intake of nourishment or excessive diarrhea, or that a disease is drying out the body.

6. Paleness in the gums is a sign of a sick puppy. A puppy's gums should be pink, or reddish-pink. When the gums are pale or white, it indicates that the puppy is malnourished because of insufficient food, disease, or parasites.

7. A dark-red or bluish tint to the skin is indicative of disease. The skin of the puppy's stomach should be a nice pink; a reddish-blue color shows that the puppy is in extreme difficulty.

8. An extremely bloated puppy may be a sick one—or one whose stomach is completely empty. Either of these conditions indicates that the puppy is in trouble. The first condition means that he is constipated or has improper elimination, which can be due to a congenital deformity at the anus. An enema is

needed (or if an anal problem, surgery) to rid the animal of the impending toxin. The bloated condition may also be caused by roundworms, and the bloat will disappear after worming. If the puppy's stomach is empty, it shows that the dam does not have enough milk, that the puppy is not getting enough milk, or that he has diarrhea which is keeping him thin.

9. Diarrhea. I would estimate that intestinal disturbances are the greatest cause of fatalities in puppies. Unless the diarrhea is checked, the puppy dehydrates and quickly dies. If there is mucus in the stools, and occasionally blood, this can be a sign of roundworms or hookworms.

Disorders of Newborn Puppies

1. Digestive trouble. One of the commonest digestive problems seen in young puppies is colicky pains after feeding, which can be due to the milk itself, too fast feeding, or possibly an irregular bowel movement involving either diarrhea or constipation.

Colic is usually caused by infections of the bowels, such as enteritis and hepatitis. There are terrible intestinal spasms which cause the puppy to cry in a pitiful way. There is usually vomiting, and the stool is loose and fetid. Palpation of the puppy causes crying and crackling pains produced by gas in the intestines. Mild enemas and milk of magnesia are sometimes beneficial. When there is severe pain, a drop of paregoric every half hour will give relief until the painful spasms stop. In diarrhea, bismuth or Kaopectate is helpful. Sometimes constipation is due to an oversight of the bitch who is supposed to lick the rectum of each puppy to prevent hardening of the bowels.

2. There is a nutritional anemia which causes death in 40 to 100 percent of some litters, usually when they are 10 to 13 days old. In this ailment the mucus membranes are pale. The best treatment is to prevent the ailment by keeping the bitch in good health, usually with adequate quantities of liver and iron, during gestation. If the mother tends to be anemic, her puppies will subsequently suffer from a similar affliction. This can be spotted by the veterinarian in his prenatal examination of the bitch, and

he will advise proper supplements before the puppies are born.

3. Another disorder in nursing puppies is staphylococcus infections. These usually develop in puppies at least a week old, and they look like puffy blisters on the body. They are caused by staphylococcus bacteria and are usually acquired by the puppies from the mammary glands and the milk. Sometimes the bitch has an infection in her vagina, and the subsequent vaginal discharge gets rubbed onto the skin of the puppies and causes the infection.

Although most of the time the puppies seem normal and nurse normally, the skin lesions spread from puppy to puppy. The sores should be washed thoroughly with an antiseptic soap, such as Phisophex, and an antibiotic ointment applied locally. In a severe case the puppy should be put on oral antibiotics, given by dropper, to prevent generalized blood poisoning.

If the bitch is the cause of the condition, her vaginal or mammary infection must be cleared up at the same time to prevent reinfection of the puppies.

4. There is an ailment in puppies called "navel ill" in which the navel cord becomes infected if dirt or other infection gets into it. This is why an antiseptic such as hydrogen peroxide or iodine should be applied to the umbilical cords.

5. Eye trouble. A puppy's eyes should begin to open at 7 to 10 days from birth. The lids part first at the inner corner and gradually extend to the outside. If the lids fail to open properly, it may be due to pus formation, which can be determined by running a finger over the lids. The best treatment is an antibiotic ointment, such as neomycin or bacitracin, placing a layer of ointment across the lids 2 or 3 times a day and working it in with the forefinger. This softens the lid, which then can usually be parted at the inner corner and drained. Don't attempt to force the lids open too soon, else the sensitive part of the lids can be injured. Gradually lids will open a bit more each day. If the eyes are neglected, the condition can result in loss of eyesight or impairment for life. The mother dog often will help open the eyes of her puppies by licking their faces, which stimulates the eyelids to part.

6. Prolapse of the rectum is occasionally seen in puppies with severe diarrhea. It is due to strain. The cause of the diarrhea must be stopped.

Early Instincts and Care

By the age of 2 weeks the puppies are roaming around the whelping box, snuggling up to one another, and sometimes even having friendly little fights. Their eyes begin to open, and although still fairly blind, and nearsighted, they begin getting about the box investigating the world that they have been born into. The bitch begins leaving the box for longer periods and returns to it only to nurse the puppies or to clean and possibly discipline them.

By the age of 21 days there is usually a decided change in the development of the puppies. Their senses are beginning to function, and their faculties, such as sight and hearing, are becoming more evident. This is the age for them to realize that there are human beings around them, and their relationships with humans should involve trust and confidence. It would leave a bad impression if they were mauled by children or adults— and with lots of noises to scare them.

After 3 weeks of age the puppies are in their learning period of development, and any experiences they undergo will affect their temperaments later in life. The first relationships, of course, are with their litter mates, and each litter has a social arrangement in which there are bullies—the larger puppies who push the small ones around—and sometimes there is an intelligent or extra-intelligent puppy who outsmarts the other puppies by always getting to the mother's breast first, or to the food dish.

After 3 weeks of age there should be a gradual weaning so that the puppies learn to eat on their own. This relieves the mother of some of her chores, which have by this time become mighty wearing on her physically. She usually begins losing weight, and her breasts are sore from the constant mauling and her puppies' sharp nails and teeth.

Any time after 3 weeks the puppies should be taught to

drink fluids. If they are well fed and the bitch has lots of milk, especially in a small litter, the puppies will be more reluctant to learn to drink outside milk. A formula (see p. 402) can be used which is beneficial to their digestive tracts. Any sudden change in diet can result in diarrhea or vomiting, and this goes for a 3-week-old puppy as well as for a 15-year-old dog.

In teaching a puppy to lap milk, dip a finger into the milk and allow the puppy to suck it, gradually taking the puppy toward a shallow saucer. Invariably he will walk into the milk and make a mess; however, this is all in the process of learning how to eat.

When puppies first begin to eat on their own, they usually take very small amounts of food, so they should be fed frequently—about 6 times a day.

After 3 weeks of age the stools of the puppies should be checked at least every 2 weeks, for worm parasites at this age are deadly. Many a fine litter has died from hookworms. Roundworms are not so dangerous but should be eliminated. If a puppy shows any worm eggs upon stool examination, he should be treated. Worms can keep the puppy unthrifty, cause digestive upsets, and in some cases lower his resistance to various diseases. At this age the animal is very fragile.

Some puppies can learn to start eating lean beef at 4 weeks of age. Rub the puppy's nose in it, and gradually he will open his mouth for it.

After 4 weeks the puppies become inquisitive and begin to investigate the whelping box and the surrounding world if they are allowed to move outside the nest. They will often begin to imitate the dam, and this is why, if the dam is a nervous one, we must take the puppies away from her after 3 weeks. As soon as they can be taught to lap milk, they should be taken away from the mother, otherwise they might assume her nervousness.

After 4 weeks of age the puppies should receive some type of serum, globulin or measles vaccine for protection.

Finally, at 6 weeks of age the puppies should be on a full diet without help from their mother.

Weaning Schedule

At 3 to 4 weeks, twice a day, feed Pablum or other cereal, from a dish. Once a day feed some type of broth—chicken or beef. Nursing by the bitch is as usual.

At 4 to 6 weeks the puppies should be fed 3 times a day with milk and cereal and possibly the addition of some dry puppy meal, in a soupy state so they can lap it up. Twice a day add more cereal and dog meal with either chicken or beef broth. The puppies will nurse as they need to, allowing the bitch to wean them gradually.

Feeding Chart for Puppies

4-6 Weeks Old

(4-6 meals a day)

Morning Meal:
> warm milk (evaporated milk preferable)
> egg
> dry cereal
>> Use 1 egg to a pint of milk. Dry cereal may include Paplum, shredded wheat, corn flakes, Pep, puffed rice, puffed wheat, Post Toasties, Zwieback, rusk, or Melba-toast.
>> If the puppy doesn't finish the meal, the bowl should be removed in a few minutes and nothing else given until the next meal.

Noon Meal:
> raw beef, chopped or ground
>> Other desirable meats are lamb, horseflesh, and veal. Fresh pork is allowed but never smoked meat, fried meat, or spicy meat. Don't feed excessive amounts of fat. Some puppies are allergic to horse meat with resultant diarrhea.

4 P.M. Meal:
> Meat
>> Any of the canned foods on the market that contain meat can be substituted for straight-meat meals. Dry dog foods are also good and can be substituted for canned foods. Most dogs like dry foods flavored with milk, meat, broth, or vegetables.

Bedtime Meal:
>   warm milk or broth
>> Give this about 10 P.M., till midnight; the puppy will sleep better and quieter. If the puppy is still hungry, you can add cereal or dog food.

Vitamins and Minerals:
>> A growing puppy needs extra amounts of cod-liver oil and calcium to build straight bones and prevent rickets. Cod-liver oil (or substitute) and calcium should be added to the food—in liquid or powder form.
>> Vegetables and tidbits from the table are good supplements to the diet so long as they are mixed with dog food.
>> *Amount to be Fed:* At your discretion. Don't overload stomach. A general rule is:

Toy Breeds:
>> At 6 weeks of age feed ¼ cup of milk and for other meals about 1 ounce of meat. Increase milk and meats in proportion to growth.

Medium-Sized Breeds:
>> At 6 weeks of age feed ½ cup of milk and cereal and 4 ounces of meat.

Large Breeds:
>> At 6 weeks of age feed 1 cup of milk for some meals and 6 ounces of meat for other meals.

The four-meals-a-day regime is continued until the puppy is about 3 months old. Gradually cut down to 3 meals a day until 6 months of age. Feed two meals a day from 6 months to 1 year of age, etc.

Barley Water Feeding

A very helpful solution that can be used to strengthen weak and debilitated puppies is a mixture made up of barley water. It has saved many a weak puppy as well as many a weak infant. This solution is easily digestible and especially good after the puppy has had diarrhea and has become very dehydrated.

To prepare, simmer 2 ounces of pearl barley in 1 quart of water for 2 hours; strain immediately to rid mixture of lumps of barley and hulls. Honey or Karo Syrup may be added to give added strength to the patient.

Behavior Patterns of Puppies

Usually the first week is mainly eating and sleeping. Then gradually the feeding periods lessen, and the play periods become more evident. Puppies growl at one another as if to tear their litter mates apart, and at times you will even notice some sexual activity, such as copulatory movements.

After 3 weeks the puppy begins to manipulate his wobbly legs and to learn the difference between his bed and his papers. This is one of the first signs of his desire to be housebroken, and the owner can help with this training process. The puppy doesn't want to lie in his own excrement and will use a different part of the whelping box to urinate and defecate. Basically this is a clean habit, but it has to be developed and helped along.

In feeding and housebreaking, regularity must be followed. The puppy expects his food at certain times, and his intestinal tract is usually attuned to these specific times. He will develop good housebreaking habits if he can depend on being taken out with the regularity.

Socialization and Transition

Most breeders call the critical period of any puppy's life the period between the ages of 21 days and 4 months. This is in regard to the development of temperament in "socialization."

Puppies raised under kennel conditions with little human contact up to 5 weeks of age will tend to show fear reactions in later life. However, if they are handled by humans after 5 weeks of age, this shy tendency can be averted. If they are not handled until they are 12 weeks of age, and they are timid and shy, it will be much more difficult to retrain them.

After 21 days the puppy starts to learn, and he needs daily periods of socialization with humans. He should be handled, played with, and treated as an individual. He should be picked up and fondled and learn how to adapt to humans.

If a puppy is removed from the litter for brief daily periods and given individual attention, and mild discipline, he will learn more easily to adjust to humans. When he finally leaves his litter for good, he will accept his new owner more readily and respond more easily to most of his owner's wishes.

A critical age is 5 to 6 weeks, and thereafter when the puppy goes to his new home. This is a traumatic change, and it should be as gentle a transition as possible. An unhappy puppyhood can leave a marked impression on temperament for the rest of the puppy's life.

6 COMMON QUERIES

SEX LIFE OF THE FEMALE

How Often Does a Bitch Come Into Heat, and How Long Does the Heat Period Last?

The normal bitch comes into heat every 6 months, and the heat period lasts 21 days, counting from the first day of bloody vaginal discharge. Some dogs don't come into heat that often, and there are dogs who come into heat every 3 or 4 months. Some dogs have "silent" heat periods, and other dogs stay in heat 4 to 5 weeks.

What Is the Correct Time to Breed a Bitch During Her Heat Cycle?

In general, the most likely time for ovulation is 9 to 14 days after the first sign of blood. A good rule of thumb is: a week coming into heat, a week of conception, and a week going out of heat. During the middle week the discharge becomes colorless, and the bitch shows a tendency to stand with her tail aside.

What Is the Best Age at Which to Breed a Bitch for the First Time?

It is best to skip the 1st heat period and breed her on the 2nd or 3rd period. She can be bred twice in a row if she is in good health and had no complications with her first litter. However, I would then skip the next heat period before breeding her again.

At What Age Should Breeding Be Terminated?

When a bitch reaches the age of 7 to 8 years, one should be cautious about breeding her and should do it only on the advice of a veterinarian. Bitches have been known to deliver puppies at 10 to 12 years of age, but this is exceptional.

At What Age Do Bitches Stop Their Heat Periods?

There is no "change of life" in female dogs. Most bitches begin having irregular heat cycles after they are 10 to 11 years old, but it is possible for them to have heat periods until 18 to 20 years of age. I would not trust such a dog out by herself; she might be attacked by a "traveling salesman."

Will a Bitch Allow Herself to Be Bred When She Is Not in Season?

No, and conception cannot take place. There are exceptions; and some bitches will attempt to copulate with a male while not in season. This is a form of nymphomania; these dogs show a false heat period and enlarged vagina, but no ovulation occurs and conception cannot take place.

Is There a Pregnancy Test for Dogs?

No, there is no laboratory test at the moment, such as the rabbit test for humans. The veterinarian can diagnose pregnancy from 3 to 4 weeks after conception by manual examination.

Are There No Birth-Control Pills or Injections for Dogs?

At present there is no birth-control pill for dogs. Human birth-control pills are not effective in dogs. Several years ago there was a hormone injection which prevented the bitch from coming into heat, but it was discovered that it predisposed dogs to uterine infections and sterility.

Can Pregnancy Be Avoided After an Accidental Mating?

Yes; there is a hormone injection which is 90-99 percent effective in preventing pregnancy if given within a week after copulation. The sooner the better! The only undesirable effect is that it prolongs the heat period for a week to 10 days.

Once a Purebred Bitch Mates with a Mongrel, Is She Ruined Forever as a Breeder of Purebred Dogs?

No. Once the womb expels its contents, there are no after-effects on future litters of puppies. This superstition, called telegony, is still widely believed. Subsequent purebred litters can be registered with the AKC.

Can a Bitch Conceive Puppies From More Than One Stud During a Heat Period?

Yes. There can be several different fathers, and this is why there are sometimes many different-looking puppies in a litter. The female dog ovulates many eggs and can be impregnated by more than one male. Thus it is wise to keep the bitch in solitary confinement after she has been bred by the dog of the owner's choice.

Is It Possible to Breed a Bitch Who Has Had a False Pregnancy?

Yes. Actually having a litter of puppies might help prevent future false pregnancies. If the bitch is not to be bred, and has had several false pregnancies, a hysterectomy is advisable.

Is There an Abnormality in the Bitch Who Has an Odd Number of Breasts?

No; there is nothing pathologically significant in an odd number of nipples. And a missing breast does not mean that the bitch will make a poor mother.

Is It Possible to Tell When a Bitch Is About to Whelp?

There is a drop in her temperature (under 100 degrees) within 24 hours of delivery. She pants and becomes nervous and restless. She scratches and tears at a rug, a bedspread, or newspapers, trying to prepare a nest. Most dogs refuse food as they approach their delivery hour. House pets say close to their masters, as they want all the attention they can get during this critical period.

How Long Should a Bitch Be in Labor Before a Puppy Is Born?

The maiden bitch with her first litter is usually in labor longer than an older and experienced dog. Generally the first puppy is born after 2 to 3 hours of labor, and then the puppies come every 10 to 15 minutes up to several hours apart. If the first puppy does not arrive within 6 hours after the commencement of labor, a veterinarian should be consulted.

If a Caesarean Operation Is Once Necessary, Will It Always Be Necessary?

Three-quarters of the dogs who have undergone Caesarean sections have had subsequent litters by the normal process of delivery. Some breeds—for example Boston bull and English bull —are more apt to need a Caesarean operation, but once a Caesarean doesn't mean always a Caesarean.

Is There a Best Age at Which to Spay a Dog?

There are conflicting opinions. I advise spaying the bitch, if she is not to be bred, just before her 1st heat period—usually around 6 months of age.

Is There an Age Limit in Spaying a Dog?
There is no age limit, but the risk increases with age. I advise spaying a bitch as soon as her breeding days are over, as this will prevent female problems in later years and reduce the incidence of mammary tumors.

Can a Dog in Heat Be Spayed?
It is better not to spay the dog in heat, as spaying at this time involves some risk because of the enlarged uterus and blood vessels. But if necessary, any competent veterinary surgeon can perform the operation.

SEX LIFE OF THE MALE

At What Age Can a Male Dog Be First Bred?
The male dog reaches puberty anywhere from 7 to 18 months of age, depending on the size of the breed; the smaller breeds mature earlier. Any time after 6 months of age he will start giving indications of sexual maturity. When he lifts his leg to urinate, he has reached "manhood." As a rule, to allow him to gain his full masculinity, it is best not to breed a dog before he is 1 year of age.

Is It True That Once a Male Dog Is Bred He Is Ruined as a Pet?
I don't think it harms a dog to breed him occasionally. Since male dogs like lovemaking once they are exposed to it, if the dog is not to be bred on a regular basis it is wise not to start in the first place.

Will Breeding a Male Dog Calm Him Down?
No; this is a fallacy. He might be calmed down temporarily after a night or two on the town, but he might also start roaming from home.

What Can Be Done With a Sexually Frustrated Male?
If the dog constantly rides people's legs or goes around the house making love to pillows, etcetera, if discipline doesn't help, castration is indicated. This will cure all his frustrations.

A castrated male dog makes an excellent pet, similar to the spayed female, as his entire life become centered on his human family.

Does a Dog, Male or Female, Need a Sex Life?

No. Many dogs have a very happy life without experiencing sex, and without being frustrated. May people think that their dogs need sex because of human frustrations. Females not to be bred I feel should be spayed for many reasons discussed before.

PUPPIES

Has Research Come Up With a Serum to Prevent Puppies From Dying the First Few Days After Birth?

In years gone by when puppies died within the 1st week of birth, death was attributed to "acid milk" in the mother. It is true that the milk of the dam can contain organisms detrimental to puppies, but it has also been discovered that there are certain diseases in puppies. "Fading" puppies' disease is caused by a virus; "septicemia of the newborn" (a blood poisoning) can be derived from an infected umbilical cord; and there are congenital defects, such as heart defect (similar to "blue" babies) and cleft palate (the puppies are unable to suck milk, and weaken and die). Digestive upsets—with diarrhea—if unattended can kill puppies within a few days. Chilling is a common environmental cause of death within the 1st week.

When a Mother Pushes a Newborn Puppy Aside and Ignores It, Does This Mean That the Mother "Knows Best" That the Puppy Is Abnormal in Some Way?

Instinctively a mother dog knows a sick or dying puppy and will usually push it off into a corner and allow it to die. But unless the puppy has a congenital defect which would make it a cripple for life, the puppy can and should be saved by hand raising.

What Is the Earliest Age at Which a Puppy Can Be Taken From Its Mother?

The earliest age is 4 weeks. That is when the puppy can

learn to drink milk out of a saucer and eat solid food.

What Is the Best Age at Which to Adopt a Puppy?

The psychologists say that the best age is 8 to 12 weeks.

At What Age Is a Dog Considered Full-Grown?

In the small breeds the dog reaches full growth at 6 months. In the medium breeds full growth is at 7 to 8 months. The large breeds grow in height until they are 12 months of age; then, until they are 2 years of age, they add muscle and weight to complete their full growth.

When Getting a Second Dog, Is It Best to Get Another Male, Another Female, or a Dog of the Opposite Sex?

In my opinion the second dog should always be of the opposite sex. With two males or two females there is a greater tendency for fights. Even though there are complications with dogs of opposite sex, the female can be put into a kennel during her season. Spaying the female or castrating the male is a solution if problems arise.

7 PUPPY CARE AND TRAINING

The formula for raising a healthy puppy is to start him off right and follow through with a good management program, which should involve the following factors: (1) proper housing; (2) proper sanitation; (3) proper nutrition; (4) control of parasites and disease; (5) proper training.

Before taking a puppy home, you should receive all necessary information about past wormings and vaccinations. Get the name of the serum or vaccine that the puppy has received so that there will be no misunderstanding. Many puppies have become victims of distemper because their owners thought that when the puppy was vaccinated at the age of 6 weeks, he received immunization for life. Likewise, some people assume that if a puppy is wormed at 6 weeks, another worm checkup will not be necessary for a year or two.

The first 6 months of a puppy's life is the most dangerous period, as he is susceptible to anything and everything, and especially to diseases and parasites. I advise the new owner to take the puppy to a veterinarian within a day or two for a thorough checkup. If there is anything wrong—for example, a congenital defect or a disease—the puppy can usually be returned, with some form of remuneration. But most important, the good health of the puppy will be ensured, and a schedule will be set up for future vaccinations and wormings.

INTRODUCTION TO THE NEW HOME

The puppy will be lonesome for the companionship of his brothers and sisters and for the warmth of his mother's breast. He will want to be cuddled. He must be treated gently, and with a minimum of noise and confusion, as he gradually becomes acquainted with his new family. He is all yours, and you are all that he has. As a dog is man's best friend, so also is man a dog's best friend.

If possible, bring the puppy home early in the day so that by nighttime he will have checked out the house. When he first arrives, he should be given some warm milk, and then light and frequent feedings. A prime mistake of new dog owners is to put down a large bowl of food and let the puppy eat all he wants. Most puppies will gorge themselves right into extreme digestive disturbances. After being made to feel secure in his oral needs, and about where he is to eat, the puppy should be shown where he will sleep, where he will exercise and where he will eliminate. He should of course, be confined to parts of the house not easily soiled.

The first 10 days are the most difficult, and since the dog is a creature of habit, he must be run on a fairly rigid schedule. He wants to be taught, and his lessons should be repeated until he gets the point.

However, no advice that I can give, or that you read elsewhere, should be hard and fast, but should be something worked out between your dog and your family. As no two dogs and no two people are alike, you will have to adjust what you read to you and your dog.

The Bed

It is wise to give the puppy a bed of his own. It gives him a sense of ownership. For an overly boisterous or destructive puppy, a shipping crate can be used. As well as serving as a bed, it will keep him confined, and as most puppies will not soil their beds, it will help in housebreaking too.

The first night or so puppies tend to be homesick but will usually settle down if taken to bed with one of the family. Unless this is to be allowed every night, however, it should be done only as a last resort; the puppy will substitute the family member for his mother and will expect a human bed the rest of his life.

Some puppies will be content in their own bed with a hot-water bottle to cuddle, or a ticking clock, or an old shoe. In severe cases a baby aspirin or a wee bit of a sleeping pill will quiet the puppy and allow everyone a good night's sleep.

HOUSEBREAKING

Most puppies are a bit nervous at first and are liable to have an accident or two. Don't be upset; be gentle and patient. In housebreaking it is up to the owner to instruct, not to condemn. Teach the puppy properly, and he will respond graciously. Don't punish him unless you are sure that you are communicating with him—that he understands what you are trying to convey to him. The dog is the closest of all animals in communication with humans; he will understand if you are explicit enough.

The average dog takes 4 to 6 weeks for complete housebreaking, but there are problem dogs and problem cases. Patience, understanding, and a ready mop are requisites. The muscles which control the bladder and intestines develop with age. Give the puppy a chance—it takes time. Success in housebreaking depends on whether you, the dog owner, can be trained. Any failure in housebreaking is usually the owner's fault.

Age to Start

Even though progress is slower with puppies under several months of age, it is never too early to start. Housebreaking may take several weeks with a puppy acquired at 6 weeks of age. Less time is required for one at 3 months. And only a few days are needed for a puppy 6 months old. Don't expect too much before 12 weeks of age; but the earlier you start, the quicker the puppy will respond.

Responsibility

Although various members of the household may help, it is best for one person to be responsible for most of the training; otherwise everyone's job soon becomes no one's job.

Supervision

Housebreaking is not a part-time task; constant supervision is necessary. The puppy must be aired upon rising, once or twice after each meal, as often as possible during the day, and especially after playing and before retiring. Dogs usually prefer to eliminate outside, and the puppy must be kept out until he has completely relieved himself. He should be praised; and if he is given a tidbit each time, the association will soon make him eliminate quickly to get his reward.

Prevention

In forming habits, an ounce of prevention is worth many pounds of correction. Watch the puppy closely. An expectant look, running back and forth to the door, and scratching at it will all indicate his needs. This is the time to get him outdoors at once. Each accident inside prolongs the housebreaking process, both by breaking down the correct habit and by providing the puppy with a place inside that he will have a tendency to use.

Regularity

Feed the puppy on a regular schedule and take careful note of his habits. Bowel movements usually occur a short time after eating. Exercise the puppy after each meal and try to get him to eliminate before allowing him back inside the house. Take him to the same area over the same route; he has a strong association for previous odors. Try to take him out at regular intervals that he can rely on, and he will soon get into the swing of things.

Some puppies stay cleaner at night if fed lightly toward evening and not fed at all after about 8 P.M. Other puppies require a feeding right before bedtime—11 to 12 P.M.—in order to stay quiet during the night. The time for the last feeding can be experimented with, earlier or later, depending on the puppy's digestive system and his ability to contain his bowel movements until morning.

Confinement

Don't allow a puppy the complete run of the house and expect him to find his way to the door each time he has to eliminate. In the daytime he should be confined to a small area where there is a linoleum surface, such as the kitchen or utility room. At night he should be confined to a small area which is well covered with newspapers. As most dogs will not soil their bedding, an older puppy who persists in having a bowel movement during the night could be confined to a small sleeping box.

Discipline

The memory of the puppy is about 30 seconds long; if he is disciplined after that time, he will not realize what he has done wrong. Try to act as quickly as possible when he errs. Either catch him in the act or take him back to the bad deed and discipline him at the spot. As soon as he has been disciplined, he should be rushed outside to the area which he is to use for elimination.

Usually scolding is adequate to show the puppy the extent to which he has fallen into disfavor. He will want to avoid such scenes. Some puppies' feelings are badly hurt at being shamed. But too, most dogs love to be praised. Be lavish with praise and petting when indicated. If scolding doesn't work, most puppies will respond to the sound of a newspaper being slapped against a hand or the floor. Persistent offenders (assuming you are not at fault) may require spanking with a rolled-up newspaper.

Paper Training

Training to newspapers may be the wisest procedure in cold weather or for people who live in apartments. Several thicknesses of newspapers are spread out on the floor, preferably on tile or linoleum. All the principles of training described above are employed except that the puppy is placed on the papers instead of outside. It is surprising how soon the puppy will want to feel the newspapers under him before eliminating. Since dogs tend to return to their own odors, some people keep one soiled newspaper to entice the puppy to the same spot. Once he knows what the papers are for, he can be taken outside on papers until he gets the idea that he is to go outside, then the papers can be discarded. Be sure to scrub immediately all mistakes with a disinfectant and deodorant (such as chlorox, pine oil or lysol) to remove odors so that the pup will not return to the scene of the crime again.

There are some excellent commercial aids for training puppies to newspapers. They have the odor of urine, which draws the puppy to the spot. Although they are helpful, they are not the total answer.

Problem Dogs

There are some problem dogs who never seem to be housebroken. In reality the dog eventually housebreaks his owner so that the owner will take him out at regular intervals.

Some spoiled dogs refuse to be housebroken, in order to punish their owners.

For certain problem dogs the discipline has to involve a certain amount of physical pain, but it should never be severe.

There are some dogs who cannot be housebroken, but not because they don't want to be. Sometimes a puppy cannot control his bladder or bowels. A veterinarian should check to make sure that infection or parasites are not causing the incontinence.

Sometimes it helps to take the puppy out with older dogs, and through imitation he learns that he is to relieve himself outdoors.

When a puppy doesn't seem to be able to get the idea of housebreaking, it is best to confine him to the kitchen as much as possible and to leave his leash on him all the time. In this way you can immediately give him a slight tug at the collar, accentuated with a firm "No!" He will soon learn that each time he makes a mistake there will be a tug and a harsh word. Take him outdoors immediately, and when he eliminates praise him as if he had performed a marvelous deed.

Some General Facts About Housebreaking

During the first 2 to 3 weeks puppies urinate and defecate in response to licking by the mother. After 3 weeks they leave the nest to urinate and defecate. By 8 to 9 weeks they localize the functions in definite spots. Normally a puppy 8 to 12 weeks of age is expected to have a call of nature every 2 hours.

Clean up the mistake carefully and take the cloth with the odor on it outdoors to the spot designated for elimination. In this way you convey to the puppy what is wanted of him. Incidentally, when puppies urinate on rugs, wash the spot out with soap and water, and then club soda, which is an excellent detergent for urine spots. A turkish towel pressed to the spot for a few hours will dry it out.

In housebreaking, don't just put a puppy out; take him out, otherwise he'll forget why he's out, and you won't know if he actually performed. Cold rain or snow shouldn't stop either of you. The puppy has a thick enough coat to be insulated against the weather.

There are some dogs who in the beginning will not relieve themselves well on a lead and have to be turned loose. This modesty should be overcome if one lives where it is dangerous to allow a dog to run. It is better for him to be constipated until he is broken from such a habit than to be killed.

As a rule females are housebroken more easily. They relieve themselves more modestly and require less shrubbery and trees than males. The male is more anxious to roam—looking for adventure and sex.

To sum it all up, feeding on schedule, regular walks, and instant scolding will quickly housebreak a puppy.

FEEDING THE PUPPY

During the first 90 days after weaning there is particularly rapid growth in the puppy and therefore the need for a high amount of protein. The extra protein enables the puppy to cope better with emergencies in his early life, such as diseases and parasites.

Proper nourishment will help the puppy's body to develop immunity against parasites, diseases, and serious infections which strike early in life.

All puppies vary in food requirements. What may be sufficient for one may be famine for another. A weaning puppy should be fed at least 5 or 6 times a day. For the 3-month-old puppy frequent feeding is advocated. From 10 weeks on he should be fed 4 meals a day, up to 4 months. Three meals daily between 4 and 6 months should be fed and 2 meals a day between 6 months and a year. After 1 year of age most dogs require only one meal a day. However, this is arbitrary. Each dog should be fed according to his needs; and the type of food and its quality must be considered in determining how many times a day to feed.

The following is a typical feeding schedule for a medium-sized breed—30 to 50 pounds at maturity. It can be altered to suit small breeds or extra-large breeds by drawing comparisons:

Age	Weight	Feedings
2 months	6-8 pounds	*Morning* 5-6 tbsp. milk 3-4 tbsp. cereal or dog food *Noon* 1-2 heaping tsp, daw ground meat or commercial canned or dry *Afernoon* Repeat morning feeding *Evening* Repeat noon feeding *Bedtime* (late evening): 5-6 tbsp. milk
3 months	10-15 pounds	Increase amounts per feeding according to puppy's growth and capacity. Gradually eliminate afternoon and bedtime feedings

4 months	15-25 pounds	*Morning*
		½-1 cup milk
		4-8 tbsp. cereal or dog food
		Noon
		4-8 heaping tbsp. raw ground meat or commercial canned or dry food
		Evening
		4-8 tbsp. meat or dog food
		3-6 tbsp. cooked mashed vegetables or table scraps
6 months	25-30 pounds	*Morning*
		¾-1½ cups milk
		¾-1½ cups cereal or dog food
		Noon
		½-1 cup meal or dog food mixed with
		¼-1 cup cereal or dry dog food
		Evening
		1-2 cups meat
		½-1 cup dog food
		½-1 cup vegetables or table scraps
8 months	about 30 pounds	*Morning*
		1½ cups milk
		toast, cereal, dog food, or dry dog food
		Evening
		2 cups meat
		cereal or toast
		vegetables or table scraps
9 months	30-40 pounds	*Morning*
		milk and cereal (2 cups each)
		Evening
		2 cups meat
		2 cups table scraps or dry dog food
10 months	40-50 pounds	*Morning*
		Milk or cereal or dog food if he will eat it. Some do not want the morning meal at this age
		Evening
		3 cups meat or dog food and vegetables or table scraps

12 months	maturity	Total amount of food—1-1¼ lbs. per day:
		1½ cups meat
		1½ cups cereal or dry dog food
		1½ cups vegetables or table scraps

The delicate digestive system of a puppy at weaning frequently requires a soft, bland diet before a regular adult ration can be tolerated. Baby cereals and baby foods are excellent.

A safe rule for frequency is "demand feeding." But don't give the puppy all he wants, as he is sure to be a glutton. Feed him all that he will digest without upsetting him. Some puppies double their weight in 2 to 3 weeks, so the quantity has to be adjusted accordingly.

The amount of food that a puppy demands depends somewhat on breed, amount of exercise, and general condition. A general rule, although arbitrary, is ½ ounce of food per pound of dog weight, per day. The dog should be fed at regular times so that he can count on and look forward to his meals.

Small breeds need more food per pound of body weight than do the large breeds. When they see a St. Bernard or a Great Dane, most people shudder to think of the food bills. But be assured that the giants eat extremely large amounts of food only during the first year or year and a half of their growth. After they have reached maturity, they don't eat much more than a collie or German shepherd. The owner of a St. Bernard or a Great Dane will feed more to his puppy the first year of his life than he will for the next 2 years.

Raw meat is more easily digested than cooked meat. Too much fat is not good for a puppy, although small amounts should be an integral part of the diet. The puppy can have most kinds of meat, such as beef, lamb, and chicken. Meat products such as liver, tripe, and kidney are beneficial additives. Horse meat is too strong for some puppies and gives them diarrhea. Egg yolks are excellent, raw or cooked, but the whites are not beneficial, especially raw.

Throughout the first year of his life the puppy should have daily amounts of vitamins and minerals added to his food. These can be in powder, liquid, or tablet form.

The health of the puppy depends on the kinds of meals that he is given every day. Fortunately the days of haphazard feeding are over. A good puppy chow prepared by a commercial company provides a basic well-balanced diet, and such a food should make up the major part of the dog's diet.

Supplements

Puppies need variety in food as well as we do, and table scraps and leftovers are an excellent means of breaking up the monotony of the everyday diet. But they should be used as a supplement and not as the main part of the diet.

Vegetables are fine for puppies and are a good food supplement. Potatoes are not injurious, as is widely believed, and within proportion are an excellent supplement. Cake, candy, and other sweets are all right to give a puppy, within reason. And incidentally, candy does not cause worms.

With their tender gums and growing teeth, most puppies enjoy gnawing on objects such as human flesh, expensive shoes, and antique furniture. The addition of kibbled food to the daily ration or the occasional large bone can provide distraction and fine therapy for teeth and gums. It should be a large beef bone, preferably a knuckle. Beef bones are all right if they are of the large variety, but rib bones or T-bones are often injurious, as they tend to break off in sharp points and cause damage to the intestinal tract. Never give small bones, such as chicken, pork, veal, lamb, or rabbit; they are injurious to throats and intestines.

Some people put chicken bones into the pressure cooker, which thoroughly softens them. Bones prepared in this way will not harm the dog, and the nutritional benefits are excellent.

Loss of Appetite

If a puppy refuses a feeding, take the food away and try again in an hour or two. If he refuses more than 2 or 3 meals, a veterinarian should be consulted, as this is a sure sign that something is wrong. A puppy must not go more than 8 hours without food; he will dehydrate, weaken, and go into shock very quickly.

Sometimes a puppy will be distracted and would rather play than eat. Keep eating and play periods separate.

Most puppies gulp their food and seldom chew it. This has nothing to do with manners and is perfectly normal. Often a puppy will regurgitate his food and then eat it again. Don't stop him from doing this no matter how distasteful it may seem to you. This is his way of predigesting his food, and is an ancestral instinct.

The Finicky Eater

There are some cuties who will hold out for filet mignon no matter what entree you put in front of them. And of course there are those who contend that the puppy will be spoiled if he is given steaks and chops and presumably will not eat commercial dog food. This may be so, but a combination of the two becomes a palatable mixture for a finicky eater.

For the finicky eater, the master must experiment and compromise. Often a puppy develops tastes which don't jibe with what the owner has in mind, and there is a constant battle of wits until either the puppy or the owner wins. A compromise is the best solution.

It may be necessary to change the diet frequently. Sometimes mix palatable table scraps with a commercial food in varying proportions. Or let the puppy miss a meal or two so that he will appreciate something he doesn't really care for (he thinks).

Overfeeding

Dogs are the most delightful beggars in the world. They love to plead for food. Don't be taken in and break down every time the dog begs. Overfeeding will result in diarrhea, vomiting, and a noisy intestinal tract.

It is not healthy for a puppy to get overweight; it puts a strain on his growing bones. It is much easier to keep his diet down than to reduce him.

Overfeeding a puppy to get a large-sized dog is not the way to do it. His size may be changed slightly—bulgingly—but heredity determines the final size of a dog and not the amount of food he is given.

Likewise, a toy-sized dog has to be bred from toy-sized parents and half-starving the dog will only make him sickly. Incidentally, the belief that feeding a puppy alcoholic beverages will stunt his growth, while widely held, has never been scientifically substantiated. (Fortunately, alcohol doesn't affect the growth rate of human creatures either.)

Don'ts

Don't allow a puppy to play or exercise strenuously immediately after eating. In some breeds, notably the Great Dane, the bloating can end in a ruptured stomach, which would be fatal.

Although a puppy should always have water handy, don't allow him to drink all he wants, especially after eating. Some puppies bloat up extensively.

Although milk is an excellent food, some puppies cannot properly assimilate it, and it gives them diarrhea. Buttermilk, however, is an excellent substitute for sweet milk and is desirable for puppies when they have a digestive upset. It restores the normal healthy bacteria to the intestinal tract during or after an illness, and it is an excellent additive during a siege of coccidiosis.

While a puppy is eating, it is best to leave him alone. And don't allow children near him. One of his ancestral instincts is to guard his food, and many a child has been bitten for getting too close to a feeding dog. Even the gentlest dog will defend his food.

Many a puppy has been poisoned by ingesting a foreign object. When you find the puppy eating something he's not supposed to, discipline him at once, and keep careful watch over him.

TEETHING

Beginning at the age of 4 months, the baby teeth (or milk teeth) fall out, allowing the adult teeth to push through the gums. By 7 to 8 months, if the baby teeth have not fallen out it is wise to have a veterinarian pull them. If they are left in, they can impede the permanent teeth and the puppy will be left with a double row of teeth or crooked teeth, which will hurt him cosmetically and in the show ring. The teeth should be taken out by a professional because if this is not done properly, they may break off at the roots and present complications in formation of the adult teeth.

Teething can cause the puppy to go off his feed, and there may be a slight diarrhea. The gums will be sore, and at such times a soft bland diet should be fed for a few days.

Most puppies like to chew on human flesh during the teething process, and it is judicious to teach them not to destroy too much of one's anatomy during this period.

TOYS

Hard-rubber toys, commercially prepared bones, and rawhide bones are fine for puppies to gnaw on, and they are soothing to sore gums and helpful in teething. Soft-rubber toys are taboo, as a puppy can quickly chew them up and the rubber that is swallowed can harm his intestinal tract.

Old neckties or several pairs of ladies' nylon hose tied together are safe and enjoyable for the puppy to play with. Toys amuse him and keep him from destroying the household.

GROOMING

Start the grooming program while the puppy is young and can be made to feel that grooming is a game. He will soon learn to look forward to being spruced up.

A soft brush is sufficient to keep most puppies in good condition. In a long-haired dog, a comb or wire brush will take care of the mats; and as he gets older a stiffer brush can be used.

In breeds that require trimming (Scotties, poodles, etc.) it is advisable to trim the heads and feet at an early age, for sanitary reasons and to get the puppy acclimated to the procedure. It must be done carefully and gently because if someone is rough during the first few trimmings, the puppy will become a problem dog and require tranquilizers for future trimmings.

It is a good idea to trim a puppy's nails also at an early age so that he will get used to it. Be careful about cutting them too close and making them bleed, since he will never forget the sharp pain. Try to make him believe that it is part of his play period—getting him to lie on his back or side. After the nails, the matted hair between toes and pads can also be cut. A puppy indoctrinated at an early age for this chore will be easy to cope with all his life. Some docile pets turn into tigers when someone attempts to trim their nails. This can usually be traced to an unhappy puppyhood experience.

Many people believe it is wrong to bathe a puppy under 6 months of age. This is not quite correct. In the summer a puppy can be bathed at an earlier age. But in cold weather one must keep the puppy from being exposed to cold and draft, as he is extremely susceptible to sore throats and colds. However, there are times when a puppy is so dirty that he needs a soap-and-water bath.

When a puppy is bathed for the first time, it must be done gently so as not to frighten him and make him forever afraid of water. Use cotton in each ear to keep out the water; and a little mineral oil or boric acid ointment in his eyes will avoid soap irritation. A mild baby soap or face soap should be used; strong flea soaps or harsh detergent soaps will dry the oils of skin and hair. After getting a good lather, rinse the puppy well, then dry him. After toweling a hair dryer can be used.

There are some excellent aerosol foam shampoos (dry shampoos) which produce suds that are lathered into the coat and skin without water. A towel is used to wipe off the excess suds. Although not quite so good as soap and water, the dry shampoos do take away a lot of dirt and can be used without worry during the winter months.

There are times when a sponge bath with a wet soapy cloth will do. Here again it should be a mild soap. Just rub the slightly damp cloth over the puppy's entire body and dry him thoroughly with towels.

For fleas or ticks, certain special puppy flea sprays and powders can be used. However, be careful of the strong flea dips used on adult dogs, as the puppy may absorb some through his skin or lick it, and it can prove fatal.

AILMENTS AND DISEASES

The commonest ailments of young puppies are vomiting and diarrhea. If a puppy vomits more than 2 or 3 times, one may well suspect that he has swallowed a foreign object. The puppy is curious by nature and will pick up and chew almost anything he comes upon. I have often had to surgically remove from puppies' stomachs or intestines such indigestible objects as golf balls, pins and needles, and razor blades, and on one occasion a diamond ring. A word of advice: if ever you are missing a small object and your puppy is vomiting, have his stomach X-rayed.

In a simple diarrhea, caused by overfeeding or teething, Kaopectate, Pepto-bismol, or bismuth (1 tsp. per 10 lbs. of puppy, 3 or 4 times a day) is soothing to the stomach and to the sensitive lining of the intestinal tract.

Intestinal parasites (worms), coccidiosis, or an infectious enteritis can be the cause of an intestinal upset, and if not treated in time can result in death.

Heavy infestation by fleas, lice, or ticks can produce anemia. Hookworms are especially serious; they suck the blood and lower the resistance to other diseases. There are efficient drugs for destroying hookworms in even very young puppies.

Coccidiosis is a disease which causes a chronic, insidious type of diarrhea. Severe cases show mucus and blood in the stools. The disease is increasing in frequency and is dangerous to the lives of puppies. Pet shops and kennels that don't practice proper sanitary procedures often spread it, as it is contagious from one puppy to another through contamination of the bowel movements.

Von Gierke syndrome, which is a condition in toy breeds, is

characterized by sudden coma, shock, and occasionally convulsions. Chihuahuas are mostly affected; Yorkshire terriers, Maltese terriers, and other small breeds also can be affected.

The cause is not completely known, although there seems to be a relationship in that stress conditions in young puppies cause hypoglycemia—a lowered level of sugar in the blood.

It can happen suddenly, without warning. The puppy is found in a semi-comatose condition with the usual signs of shock, such as pale gums and tongue, and dilated and unfocused eyes. The animal sometimes screams in pain.

Immediate attention is required to save the puppy. Karo syrup, molasses, or any other form of sugar should be poured slowly into the puppy's mouth. Stimulants, such as brandy, and warmth should be provided.

Any predisposing factor that causes lack of appetite, and no food for over 8 hours, can produce the syndrome (a puppy cannot go over 8 hours without food or water). Young toy puppies that are handled much or become exhausted are prone to this disorder. After an accident, illness, or any traumatic experience, force-feed the puppy with broth or eggnog.

Rickets is a condition of puppies caused by a deficiency of the minerals calcium and phosphorus. The minerals are helped in absorption by the presence of vitamins A and D.

Symptoms of rickets are bowed legs with large knots of bone at the leg joints. There are also knots of bone on the ribs. It is diagnostic to see a puppy with his toes spread in an awkward position and his legs bent at his carpal (wrist) joints.

Although any breed is susceptible to rickets, it is usually seen in fast-growing breeds, such as the Great Dane and German shepherd.

A deficiency of vitamins and minerals will also keep a puppy's ears from standing erect in such breeds as the boxer, Doberman, and Great Dane.

If a puppy does a lot of hiccupping, fear not. This is normal —spasms of the diaphragmatic muscle which occur at various times in the growing period. There is no pathological significance.

Signs of a Sick Puppy

—Vomiting
—Diarrhea
—Loss of appetite
—Lethargy, lassitude, listlessness
—Coughing
—Running eyes and nose
—High fever

Safety Rules for Puppies

—Give only large beef-knuckle bones
—Keep dangerous objects off the floor and out of reach
—Never, never worm a sick puppy
—Children should not be allowed to maul a young puppy
—Don't allow a puppy freedom of the outdoors if there is any danger from automobiles

EXERCISE, BEHAVIOR, TRAINING

Exercise

Overfeeding and insufficient exercise are the principal causes of fat, lazy, sluggish puppies; and this goes for adult dogs too. The dog's body is geared for running and playing, and both are necessary for his well-being. Lack of exercise can bring on all kinds of digestive disorders and physical and mental sluggishness. Playing with other dogs and humans provides physical and emotional gratification. A long walk with your puppy, besides being physically beneficial to both of you, is pleasing to his ego.

A puppy should be taken out every 2 hours, if possible, but at least 3 times a day. Walking with your dog should be a period of enjoyment as well as serious training for his future well-being. The earlier you leash-train him, the better. Teach him to walk a few steps in front of you, not constantly pulling on the leash.

I don't advise leashing or tying a puppy outdoors by himself for a long time. He may become entangled in the leash or rope and injure himself. An outdoor pen or a fenced-in area is desirable so he can have some freedom on his own and be outdoors when the weather permits. Some shelter should be provided in case of rain or on hot sunny days for shade. He should also have an ever-present pan of water. Some dogs prefer to be with humans and don't wish to stay outside by themselves. They should not be kept outside if they don't wish to stay, and certainly not in wet or cold weather especially if they are toy or small puppies.

Leash Training. A certain amount of psychology is needed in teaching the puppy to be towed along with a leash attached to his neck. Don't expect the puppy to walk along at your side the first time. Invariably he will fight and tug and pull.

The first step is to teach the puppy to wear a collar. Any time after 6 weeks of age a light collar can be put on him. He will not like it and will scratch at it and try to get it off but will soon resign himself to his fate.

Allow him to get used to the collar for a week or so, and then attach a short length of rope to the collar and let him play with it and drag it around the house. Occasionally pick up the rope and hold it so that he knows you have control of his collar. At first he will pull and tug and try to go in every direction. Don't jerk it, and he will soon realize that nothing drastic will happen to him when you hold the rope. He will get to like your playing with him—catching the rope.

The next step is to teach him to walk with you without getting under your feet. Repeat the lesson 2 or 3 times a day; just before mealtime is preferable because he will get a reward when it's over.

Behavior

There is an old saying, like master, like dog, and a disobedient or neurotic dog is often the result of poor training. There is a ring of truth to the statement that neurotic dogs are the result of neurotic owners. However, I don't wish to imply that all neurotic dogs have emotionally unstable owners.

Puppies are great imitators, and a shy or timid dog is often reflecting those tendencies of his owner. Also, it is well to choose a puppy's companions wisely. If there are any with bad faults, keep the puppy away as you would keep a child away from a juvenile delinquent.

Good kennel owners give their puppies daily individual care. It has been proved that dogs that are raised in isolation with no human contact develop emotional imbalances that interfere with normal development.

Infantile autism, commonly called kennelitis, is often seen in dogs left in kennels without human love. It is characterized by excessive shyness and introspection and is brought on more by environment than by heredity. Some of these dogs become fearful of everyone but their owners and develop fear-biting.

There is also a tendency for this to happen when a puppy receives too much love and affection from one person. The puppy becomes so attached to the person that he growls at or bites anyone else. Such puppies don't have enough contact with the outside world and distrust the human race.

I advise all dog owners to take their puppies with them on trips around town so that the puppies can see all shapes and sizes of human beings. It will show them that people are not out to harm them—that many people love dogs and will stop and compliment and pat them. A puppy should make friends with strangers, up to a point.

Most destructive dogs do their bad deeds out of boredom. They are not necessarily juvenile delinquents if they chew and destroy things. This is part of the development stage in normal, healthy puppies. Before leaving a puppy alone in the house, it is a good idea to take him for a long walk—tire him out—so he will nap while you are out. This also works well when taking a puppy on a car trip.

Training

Often I'm asked which breed is best for training. Although we see more poodles and German shepherds in obedience trials today, this doesn't necessarily mean that they are the smartest and most trainable. It just means that there are more of them. There is much convincing evidence that every breed is capable of doing well in obedience training, and that no one breed has a monopoly on brains. There are no "stupid" dogs. It is up to each owner to bring out his dog's inherent intelligence.

Each puppy is an individual in mentality and adaptability, and each master must supply the supervision that is needed to mold the development of the puppy's character and disposition. Some puppies are bold and some are shy, but the majority seem to be undecided which way they are going to develop.

Teaching the puppy his name is one of the first things to concentrate on. Pick a simple-sounding name and use it as much as possible every time you talk to him and with every command. He soon will learn that the word is his. When you call him and he comes to you, praise him, pat his head, and give him a tidbit. He should associate his name with something pleasant.

Start the training gently and tenderly and with much patience. Treat him as you would a child, with sympathy and understanding. Lavish upon him all the love that he deserves, and also the discipline that he deserves when he does wrong.

Don't be harsh with him. Yelling, cussing, kicking, and beating will not hurry up his training and more likely will deter him from the one and only desire in life, to please you, his loving master.

Don't expect miracles overnight. The puppy learns by repetition, and you must develop communication for complete and worthwhile training. Talk to him, explain to him and show him what you want. If he can't seem to learn something, teach him something else that he can do. He wants to learn, but we all have our limitations. Once you start teaching him something, keep repeating it until he understands completely.

The first rule in training is to make all lessons brief and interesting so that the puppy will not become bored.

In a training program rewards and discipline should be given immediately. Be lavish in your praise; it is important to the dog's ego to be complimented. Usually a disgusted voice is discipline enough. If something more forceful is needed, a rolled-up newspaper should be sufficient. Most dog trainers say the hand should never be used in punishment; and I certainly don't advise striking a dog on the head or backbone, as these are delicate areas. A light thump on the fanny or the sides will get the point across.

Dogs don't understand words as words. They associate certain sounds with certain commands and get to learn what they must do when they hear the sounds. Actually, I have a number of patients who do seem to understand words and whose owners have to spell out certain words that they don't want the dogs to hear.

There are some basic commands that every puppy should be taught The most important command for the dog to understand is "No!" You have to make him know you mean it. "Quiet" should also be taught early in his life —and he should stop his noise immediately.

Training Rules—

—The best time for training the puppy is before he is fed, so that he will be looking forward to the reward of a good meal.

—For a satisfactory training program the puppy should have complete confidence in you.

—Never train a puppy while you are in a bad mood or have lost control of your emotions. Especially don't lose patience and kick a puppy in anger or throw things at him. He is still a babe in arms and cannot be expected to grasp everything at once.

—Allow only one member of the family to teach him commands and tricks. Once he has learned them all thoroughly, then others can help.

—Always talk to a dog before you approach him. This goes for any dog. Let him know you are his friend.

—Don't confuse a puppy by giving him inconsistent commands.

—Don't punish the dog with a training lead or other training object, or he will become fearful of training.

—Don't allow the training periods to get so long that the puppy becomes tired or bored.

—A puppy should never be picked up by his ears—as one of our Presidents found out, much to his chagrin.

Dos and Don'ts of Training

Dos

1. *Do* have only one, and the same, person in charge of the training program. More than one person giving commands can confuse the dog and make learning more difficult. Once the dog has learned all the commands, other members of the family can contribute to further training.

2. *Do* train the dog at the same time and place each session. Continuity and familiarity aid in the learning process.

3. *Do* be patient, kind, and gentle. The younger the dog, the easier and shorter the training sessions should be. They should be no longer than five minutes in the beginning. You can gradually increase the intensity and length (but never longer than 15-20 minutes) of the sessions as the commands are learned.

4. *Do* use the same tone of voice when giving commands. Shouting and screaming only confuse and deter learning.

5. *Do* be consistent with your commands so the dog will know what you are striving for. Use the same words and signals. Proceed with a new command only after the dog has learned previous commands.

6. *Do* use a training collar in the initial teaching of commands. As the dog learns, the learning will be reinforced with off-lead sessions.

7. *Do* reward and punish. Praise him when he follows instructions; indicate your displeasure when he doesn't. Let him know you are serious.

8. *Do* play with the dog after the training sessions as a sort of reward for his serious concentration.

Don'ts

1. *Don't* attempt to train a dog after meals or exercise. The dog will be sluggish both mentally and physically.

2. *Don't* make the training sessions long. Start with five minutes and gradually extend them to 15-20 minutes as the dog matures.

3. *Don't* expect miracles. It takes a minimum of four lessons to learn a command, and some dogs take longer.

4. *Don't* lose your patience. Shouting and screaming only confuse the dog.

5. *Don't* hit the dog in a fit of temper. If scolding is needed, be sure he understands why. Talk to him and try to explain his deficiencies.

6. *Don't* proceed with a new command until he has mastered the one you are attempting to teach. It will only confuse him.

7. *Don't* use a spiked training collar to try to impress commands on a dog. Cruelty does not help obedience training.

8. *Don't* allow playing during the sessions. Be serious. Make him realize that you mean business.

9. *Don't* reward him with a tidbit for each successful response. He'll be spoiled into expecting such a reward. Praise is enough. Tidbits can be given at the end of the training session.

10. *Never, never* let a training session end with the dog getting his own way or he will believe he can lead you. It must end only when he has followed a command and you have proven your authority and leadership.

INDEX